THE NATIONAL INSTITUTE OF
ECONOMIC AND SOCIAL RESEARCH

Occasional Papers
XLII

BRITISH IMPORTS OF CONSUMER GOODS

A study of import penetration 1974–85

BRITISH IMPORTS OF CONSUMER GOODS

A study of import penetration 1974–85

ANN D. MORGAN

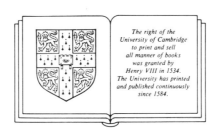

The right of the
University of Cambridge
to print and sell
all manner of books
was granted by
Henry VIII in 1534.
The University has printed
and published continuously
since 1584.

CAMBRIDGE UNIVERSITY PRESS

CAMBRIDGE

NEW YORK   NEW ROCHELLE   MELBOURNE   SYDNEY

Published by the Press Syndicate of the University of Cambridge
The Pitt Building, Trumpington Street, Cambridge CB2 1RP
32 East 57th Street, New York, NY 10022, USA
10 Stamford Road, Oakleigh, Melbourne 3166, Australia

First published 1988

Printed in Great Britain at The Bath Press, Avon

British Library cataloguing in publication data
Morgan, Ann D.
British imports of consumer goods: a study
of import penetration 1974–85. –
(Occasional papers/National Institute of
Economic and Social Research; 42).
1. Great Britain – Commerce – History –
20th century   2. Commercial products –
Great Britain
I. Title   II. Series
382'.45   HF1040.9.G7

Library of Congress cataloguing in publication data

Morgan, Ann D.
British imports of consumer goods: a study of import penetration
1974–85/Ann D. Morgan.
p.   cm. – (Occasional papers/the National Institute of
Economic and Social Research: 42)
Includes index.
ISBN 0 521 35349 1
1. Great Britain – Commerce.   I. Title.   II. Series: Occasional
papers (National Institute of Economic and Social Research); 42.
HF3506.5.M67   1988
382'.5'0941 – dc19   87–25662 CIP

ISBN 0 521 35349 1

For E.V.M.

CONTENTS

TABLES

ix

SYMBOLS IN THE TABLES
... not available
— nil or negligible
n.a. not applicable

CHARTS

ACKNOWLEDGEMENTS

I should like to thank the Leverhulme Foundation who financed the research on which this book is based, and without whose generosity it would never have been written. Likewise it would never have been written but for the help given by the many people who patiently and instructively discussed the reasons for import penetration in the consumer goods market and replied to questionnaires. I am deeply grateful to all of them. It is not possible to mention them by name for it would be a breach of confidence and, besides, the list would run to several indigestible pages; but I must mention the help that I received from the National Chamber of Trade and its members. Its extent will be plain to anyone who reads Chapter 4. Finally, I should like to thank my colleagues at the National Institute for their assistance, especially Darinka Martin who ploughed her way through countless company reports as well as collecting other statistics, and to Carol Savage and Julia Salisbury who handled the preparation and despatch of the questionnaires.

National Institute of Economic ADM
   and Social Research
London
June 1987

INTRODUCTION

OBJECT OF THE STUDY

This project was first undertaken in the belief that, while there has been a great deal of work relating to the competitiveness of United Kingdom exports and the effects of high costs and technical weakness on overseas sales, less attention has been paid to the parallel issues of growing import penetration except, of course, by those immediately affected. The object of the research presented here was to examine the influence of price and non-price factors on import penetration of the market for non-food consumer goods in the United Kingdom. Besides such non-price factors as are loosely covered by the term 'design', it was proposed to consider the effect on imports of membership of the European Community (EC), of the activities of multinational enterprises both British and foreign, of the distributive system, and of marketing and consumer preference.

What goods are offered to the final consumer is in large measure determined by the initial buyers of those goods, that is by the distributive trades and more especially by retailers. It is they who weigh up 'value for money' in a fashion not open to any individual consumer and who are best placed to determine the relative merits and demerits of British and foreign goods so far as the final purchaser is concerned. It appeared therefore that if retailers could be persuaded to discuss their reasons for buying imports rather than domestically-produced goods, the findings of any research would be enriched and some headway might be made in assessing the importance of those elusive non-price factors such as 'design' in competition. It was this that was the deciding factor in choosing consumer goods as the subject for study. The research was confined to non-food manufactured consumer goods, because trade in food is covered by different rules, while production and distribution are, at least to some extent, handled by different types of organisation.

It should be emphasised from the outset that the decision to concentrate on import penetration, rather than the competitiveness of British relative to foreign products in general, does not imply any value judgement that a high degree of import penetration is undesirable; that for a British consumer to purchase imported manufactures is 'bad', to purchase domestic products 'good'. On the contrary: the growth of imports has effectively increased consumers' real income and vastly widened the

range of goods available. The choice of import penetration as the subject
of research was, to a great extent, a matter of convenience. With limited
resources it would have been impossible to ask many foreign purchasers
why they bought British rather than foreign goods or vice versa. More-
over, growing import penetration and relative export decline are two
sides of the same coin so that examining one should throw light on
the other, although it is not true that because a given product sells well
at home it will sell equally well abroad. The idiosyncrasies of national
and local taste alone would prevent that. Indeed, it is one of the problems
facing British consumer goods industries that, having developed to cater
largely to English-speaking markets abroad as well as at home, they
now operate within the framework of an economic community with a
very different cultural background, different social habits and different
purchasing patterns.

Surprisingly enough, little reference was made in interviews to the
effect of membership of the EC on United Kingdom imports, perhaps
because memories are short and it was water under the bridge. It did
enhance the opportunities for European exporters to this market in the
mid-1970s, but even then, and to a far greater degree in subsequent
years, other factors have been more important in fostering the growth
of import penetration by goods from Continental Europe. Most commonly, references to the Community were coupled with the remark that
British manufacturers were neglecting their opportunities there, a matter
outside the scope of this study. Much less emphasis than was initially
expected has therefore been given to the effects of EC membership.

Similarly, there was little reference to the effect of multinational firms'
operations on imports. Where the multinationals were important, their
trade affected both exports and imports, tending to increase the level
of both. Their role in certain industries where they are present in force
is examined, but in general it appears that their influence is slight outside
the electrical and electronics industries.

Inevitably there were other shifts in emphasis as the research pro-
gressed, particularly towards more extended consideration of the retailing
of consumer goods. In part this was because there has apparently been
so little analysis of developments in retailing, other than food retailing,
that it seemed that any addition to the meagre information available
would be intrinsically valuable; in part because of the belief of manufacturers and retailers alike that the pattern of retailing in the United
Kingdom had contributed to the growth of import penetration.

THE DEFINITION OF CONSUMER GOODS

One problem that arose at an early stage is that, in practice, there is
no such thing as a purely consumer goods industry. There are simply

industries that sell a greater or lesser proportion of their output via the retail system to the final consumer. A typical consumer good, say a teacup and saucer, may be sold to the consumer for use in the home; equally, it may be sold to hotels, restaurants and canteens, to hospitals, to schools, and so on. What is essentially a capital good, for example cement or a portable power tool, may be sold to the consumer for use in his home. The packaging will be different but the goods may be identical, although it is more likely that they will differ in certain important respects and be produced by specialised firms. But they will still be the product of the same industry.

The 1979 input–output table tries to distinguish sales by all industries, grouped under 88 heads, to each other and to the various sectors of final demand. In ten groups, soap and toilet preparations, electronic consumer goods, domestic electric appliances, knitwear, carpets, footwear, clothing, household textiles and soft furnishings, wood furniture, and miscellaneous manufactures including toys and sports goods, 30 per cent or more of total supplies (domestic production plus imports) was sold to the consumer. His share was highest in domestic electric appliances where consumer spending accounted for an estimated 73 per cent of total supplies; the median share was just under 50 per cent. In a number of other groups, one industry or even part of one industry was obviously an important supplier to the consumer. These also were included in the definition of consumer goods industries, provided that it was possible to obtain some kind of match between figures of output and trade. Together the consumer goods industries so defined accounted for some 85 per cent of relevant expenditure. The latter was defined as consumers' expenditure on goods other than food, drink and tobacco, books, tapes and the like, and vehicles, or spending on goods distributed principally by food retailers such as cleaning materials. A list of the industries concerned will be found in Appendix 1.

A DIGRESSION ON STATISTICS

The attempt to arrive at a workable definition for consumer goods industries introduces another problem, that of the statistics available. There are endless difficulties, of classification, of continuity, of accuracy and coverage. Broad differences in classification between data on production and trade arise partly from international practice, the use of the standard industrial classification (SIC) for one and the standard international trade classification (SITC) for the other. The United Kingdom statistical authorities reclassify figures of total trade according to the SIC, but for any more detailed information one must use the SITC. At any level finer than that of the four-digit industry the two are incompatible. This difficulty may be unavoidable, but others are not. At the level of specific products, the use of different definitions and units of measurement may make comparisons between domestic production and trade impossible. It is hard to understand why some products are defined in the same fashion in both production and trade data while others are not, or why some are expressed in the same quantity units while others differ. How, for example, can one compare a ton of imported sheets with thousands of domestically-produced sheets?

Again, apart from rather broad indicators, it is difficult to find consistent series that extend back over more than a few years. The trade figures were revamped in 1978, a new SIC classification was adopted in 1980, the size of firm, measured by employment, covered by the quarterly enquiries was drastically reduced in a number of industries in 1981 and the classification and coverage of the Retail Enquiry seems to alter every time it is undertaken. Usually the changes introduced represent an improvement, though not always, as witness the case of the quarterly enquiries; but only rarely is any linkage or overlap between the old and the new provided, as anyone who attempts to use the data will quickly discover.

The hapless user is presented with a mass of detailed information, that may or may not be published on a regular basis, whose value is hard to discern and whose accuracy is suspect. Many of the bodies representing particular industries believe that there are serious errors in the statistics; those who collect their own figures can produce chapter and verse. It would be absurd to ask for complete accuracy in the data collected, but if less detail were required, accuracy might be improved. Less data with greater consistency would certainly increase the usefulness of published figures.

PLAN OF THE BOOK

This is by the way. To return to the subject of import penetration in the consumer goods market, the results of the research are organised as follows. Chapter 2 provides a broad general survey of developments in demand, output and trade in the consumer goods industries from 1974 to 1985. Chapter 3 covers developments in non-food retailing over a slightly shorter period, beginning in 1976, the year of the first Retail Enquiry. (There was a five-year gap between it and the last Census of Distribution.) Chapter 4 summarises the findings of questionnaires sent to retailers and used in interviews. The questionnaires relate to specific products or product groups, but the consistency in the replies was such that it seemed useful to provide a summary of this kind, as well as using them when discussing particular industries. Furthermore, some of the questionnaires covered products not considered in any detail elsewhere.

The four following chapters are case studies of certain aspects of the clothing and knitwear industries (treated together because they are sold together to meet the same demand), domestic electric appliances, household textiles and furniture. The case studies are intended to illustrate the different ways in which import penetration affected specific consumer goods industries and to show the different kinds of import competition faced in different markets. They also cover the structure of manufacturing and retailing, relations between manufacturers and retailers, and changes that are emerging; and retailers' views of British and imported products and producers, and their reasons for purchasing imported rather than domestically-produced goods. Chapter 9 deals with some of these points in relation to three relatively successful industries, toiletries, domestic china and earthenware and wallcoverings, seeking for any factors common to the three which make for a better-than-average performance. Chapter 10 summarises the findings of the study and considers some policy implications. As is often the case, it suggests the need for further research, particularly into the structural relationship between industry and its customers; for the case studies demonstrate that the idea of a 'market' inhabited by producers and consumers of similar size and strength is very wide of the mark when it comes to consumer goods in the United Kingdom.

2

THE CONSUMER GOODS INDUSTRIES 1974–85

THE DEMAND FOR MANUFACTURED CONSUMER GOODS

This chapter is intended to provide a broad picture of what happened to output and trade in the consumer goods industries from 1974 to 1985, by way of background to the case studies of specific industries in later chapters. Looking at data on import penetration and production in isolation encourages the conclusion that almost all the troubles of British consumer goods industries have arisen from the growth of imports, especially during the 1980s. In common with the rest of British industry, however, manufacturers of consumer goods have suffered from wide fluctuations in the rate of growth of domestic demand over the past fifteen years and more, fluctuations that in themselves may help to explain the growth of import penetration. It is appropriate, therefore, to begin by considering how demand for this particular group of products has developed.

The consumer boom that ushered in the 1970s was abruptly halted in late 1974 by the oil price rise. There followed several years of stagnation which lasted until 1978 when demand again rose steeply. This boom was shortlived, halted by the second oil price rise, once again followed by stagnation, and in 1983 a renewed rise in demand that still continues. Demand for manufactured consumer goods followed a similar course; but for the purposes of the present study, it is convenient to distinguish two periods of equal duration (1974 to 1979 and 1979 to 1984) because of the remarkably similar pattern of demand growth. In both, an initial fall in real spending on manufactured consumer goods was followed by stagnation and then two years of lavish spending. The increase in outlays from 1974 to 1979 was rather larger than the increase from 1979 to 1984 (16 per cent in real terms against 14.5 per cent) because of a bigger rise in spending from 1977 to 1979 than from 1982 to 1984; the annual average rate of increase in other years hardly differed between the two periods, as may be seen from table 2.1.

This pattern was broadly repeated in different sectors, but with significant differences in average rates of growth, particularly after 1979. Spending on electrical and electronic goods has grown faster almost throughout the period, because of the public's huge appetite for electronic consumer goods; even in 1980 and 1981 demand barely faltered. Demand for

Table 2.1. *Rates of change in consumers' real expenditure on manufactures*

Annual average, per cent

		Clothing and footwear	Electrical and electronic goods[a]	Other household goods[b]	Other goods[c]	Total
1974–9		3.9	4.5	2.5	1.4	3.0
of which:	1974–7	1.2	−0.5	−0.8	−0.2	0.1
	1977–9	8.2	12.6	7.6	3.7	7.5
1979–84		3.0	9.0	0.2	1.1	2.7
of which:	1979–82	0.5	5.8	−1.6	−1.7	0.2
	1982–4	6.9	13.9	3.0	5.5	6.7
1984–5		6.9	12.4	3.6	4.1	6.5

Source: United Kingdom National Accounts, 1986 edition.
[a] Including gas appliances and photographic equipment.
[b] Furniture, carpets, household textiles and soft furnishings, hardware, etc., DIY goods.
[c] Sports goods and toys, pharmaceutical products (excluding NHS payments), toilet articles, jewellery and miscellaneous.

clothing and footwear has consistently grown rather faster than total demand; but with the exception of a few specific categories such as DIY goods, toys and sports goods, consumer spending on other household goods and miscellaneous manufactures fell particularly sharply after 1979, and in the case of such luxury goods as jewellery has yet to recover to the 1979 level. Thus, underlying the fluctuations in total demand, there has been a shift of expenditure away from the more traditional household and luxury items towards new categories of leisure goods and, to a lesser extent, clothing, which has taken its toll of the industries concerned.

The effect of the fall in final consumer demand on output after 1979 was exacerbated by sustained destocking at the retail level. Retail stocks were cut back during both 1975 and 1980, but in the earlier period they were rebuilt in the two years following 1975 while destocking continued in 1981 and 1982, although at a reduced rate. Total retail stocks showed a net increase of £697 million, measured at 1980 prices, from the end of 1974 to the end of 1977, and a decrease of £720 million from 1979 to 1982. The former offset probably three quarters or more of the fall in final consumers' expenditure on all goods in the earlier period; the latter added some 20 to 25 per cent to the decline in spending during 1980 to 1982. (The exact size of the effect is uncertain because of changes in the incidence of VAT.) The effect on the demand for manufactured consumer goods as they are defined here was probably greater still. The fall in stocks held by retailers of mainly non-food consumer goods between the end of 1979 and 1982 was of the order of £660 million at 1980 prices,[1] about four times as large as the very modest rise in actual consumer spending on these goods between 1979 and 1982. Comparable figures are not available for earlier years; but since manufactured consumer goods accounted for 90 per cent of retail destocking from 1979 to 1982, it may be supposed that they accounted for around 90 per cent of the end-1974 to end-1977 rise. This would have meant that demand rose by 3 per cent over the period rather than a mere 0.2 per cent. Taking stock changes into account, the pattern as well as the size of demand growth was less favourable to producers from 1979 to 1984 than it had been in the preceding five years. Any fall in demand between 1974 and 1979 was fairly rapidly reversed; because of the very big drop from 1979 to 1980 it took four years for consumer spending plus retail stockbuilding to surpass the 1979 level.

THE GROWTH OF TRADE AND OUTPUT

The available data on the volume of trade in consumer goods cover a narrower range of products than the expenditure data, but they probably reflect the general trend well enough. Figures for the same periods as in table 2.1 are shown in table 2.2. The volume of imports rose almost without interruption from 1974 to 1984, save for slight falls in 1975 and 1982, and grew very much faster than consumer spending. When demand surged, as in 1977–9 and 1982–4, the rate of import growth quickened but, curiously enough, it was lower in relation to the growth of consumer spending than during periods of slack demand. From 1979 to 1982, for example, when real spending rose by 0.2 per cent annually, imports rose by 3.7 per cent annually; from 1982 to 1984 the annual rates of increase were respectively 6.7 and 11 per cent. A great deal of the increase in total consumer goods imports is self-propelled, so to speak, and has occurred regardless of the state of demand.

The most rapid increase in import volume was in electrical and electronic consumer goods, in line with the growth of demand in this sector; but the rise in the volume of imports of miscellaneous goods (a mixture of household goods and leisure products) was almost as large proportionately from 1974 to 1984, though demand grew notably less throughout. In 1985, the total volume of imports was unchanged on 1984, entirely because of a fall in imports of clothing and footwear. The volume of other goods imported rose again, if modestly by comparison with the two previous years.

Imports behaved in similar fashion during 1974 to 1979 and 1979 to 1984. Export behaviour changed radically, and the cyclical pattern disappears. From 1974 to 1977 exports in all sectors rose faster than

Table 2.2. *Rates of change in the volume of trade in manufactured consumer goods*[a]

Annual average, per cent

	Clothing and footwear	Electrical and electronic goods	Other goods[a]	Total
Imports				
1974–9	10.5	6.7	10.4	9.6
of which: 1974–7	7.0	3.6	6.0	5.9
1977–9	15.9	11.4	17.4	15.3
1979–84	4.3	10.8	7.1	6.6
of which: 1979–82	1.6	7.0	4.1	3.7
1982–4	7.7	16.8	12.8	11.0
1984–5	−4.9	4.1	1.7	0.0
Exports				
1974–9	12.1	0.5	6.5	6.1
of which: 1974–7	20.0	6.5	9.5	10.6
1977–9	0.9	−8.0	2.1	−0.3
1979–84	0.2	−8.5	3.1	0.7
of which: 1979–82	−1.1	−13.4	−1.9	−3.5
1982–4	2.2	−0.6	12.3	7.4
1984–5	6.9	14.2	2.9	3.5

Source: Monthly Review of External Trade Statistics.
[a] Excludes certain major consumer goods (carpets, household textiles, china and glass, cutlery, stoves etc., soap and toilet preparations) but includes other miscellaneous items not covered in table 2.1. Coverage of clothing and footwear and of electrical and electronic goods is broadly similar to that in table 2.1.

imports; from 1977 to 1979 they faltered; and in the following three years fell sharply. Once again the most extreme movement was in electrical and electronic goods, where the volume of exports fell by almost half between 1977 and 1982. It dropped again in 1983, but then staged a remarkable recovery, though it remains far below the peak levels of the mid-1970s. The volume of clothing and footwear exports also touched bottom in 1983, but exports of other consumer goods began to recover in that year and surged ahead in 1984. By 1985, the volume of all consumer goods exports was some 4 per cent higher than its previous peak in 1978.

Table 2.3 shows rates of change in the volume of output of a broad range of manufactured consumer goods. The familiar cyclical pattern reappears, of three years stagnation followed by two years growth during both 1974 to 1979, and 1979 to 1984. On average, however, the rate of growth was extremely modest in the first period and negative in the

Table 2.3. *Rates of change in output of manufactured consumer goods*

Annual average, per cent

	Clothing, footwear, etc.[a]	Durables[b]	Other consumer goods[c]	Total
1974–9	0.9	−1.3	1.1	0.4
of which: 1974–7	0.9	−2.0	0.4	−0.2
1977–9	1.0	−0.2	2.3	1.3
1979–84	−2.4	−2.9	−0.8	−1.7
of which: 1979–82	−6.4	−7.4	−4.0	−5.4
1982–4	3.9	4.3	4.2	4.2
1984–5	3.7	3.0	3.2	3.2

Source: *United Kingdom National Accounts*, 1986 edition; *Monthly Digest of Statistics.*
[a] Including household textiles, canvas and leather goods.
[b] Electrical and electronic goods, furniture, carpets, etc., jewellery, watches and clocks, etc.
[c] Covers a variety of products in addition to sports goods and toys.

second, so that even by 1985 output was well below the level of the late 1970s. Production of durable goods was most seriously affected, because of the importance of electrical and electronic goods in this group. The miscellaneous group put up the best performance but its apparent success may simply reflect the coverage of the index. It includes some industries such as newspaper publishing which, of their nature, are little affected by foreign trade and less susceptible to fluctuations in demand than manufactured consumer goods in general.

Chart 2.1 compares movements in total demand (consumers' expenditure on manufactured consumer goods adjusted for stock changes on the assumption that 90 per cent of changes in retail stocks affected manufactured consumer goods) with changes in output and in net imports, that is imports less exports, measured at constant 1980 prices. From 1974 to 1979 the three moved broadly together, and the growth of domestic demand was the prime influence on production. In 1980 net imports rose while demand and output fell, and from 1980 to 1982 output continued to fall while both demand and imports rose. Thereafter all three turned up again, though with output rising more slowly than the other two. What requires explanation is the continuing fall in output after the recession in demand had ended, and the persistent tendency of net imports to rise faster than demand ever since 1977. These points are discussed in relation to specific products in the case studies. Here, however, something may be said about the general influence of changes in relative prices.

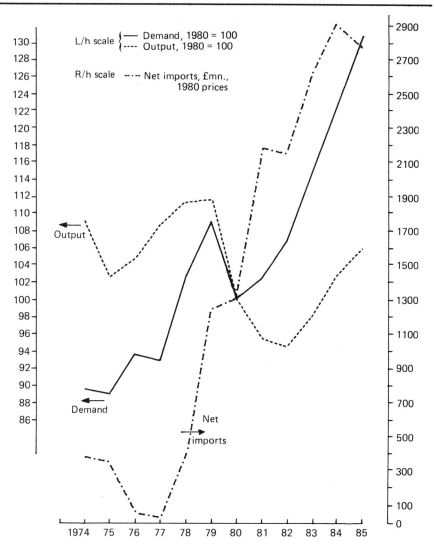

Chart 2.1   Consumer goods: demand, output and net imports

THE INFLUENCE OF RELATIVE PRICES

There is no official index of domestic producer prices of consumer goods in the United Kingdom, but by weighting together the published series for different industries one may be devised. This was done using 1980 import values as weights, and the resultant index compared with the import unit value index for consumer goods to give an index of relative United Kingdom prices. From 1974 to 1976, the index fell by 6.5 per

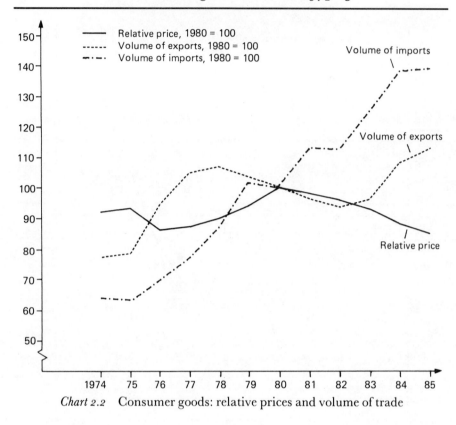

Chart 2.2   Consumer goods: relative prices and volume of trade

cent. It then turned up, at first gradually but after 1978 at an accelerating rate, rising by 16 per cent to 1980. Thereafter it fell, again at an accelerating rate. Other things being equal, and allowing for a time lag of one to two years, the volume of exports should therefore be expected to rise up to 1978, fall to 1982 and then rise again, while imports moved inversely.

What actually happened is shown in chart 2.2, where the index of relative prices is plotted alongside indices for the volume of exports and imports. Exports moved according to expectations, following relative prices with a lag of two years. The volume of imports was apparently impervious to changes in relative prices throughout the period. In the mid-1970s the rise in imports, despite a fall in relative prices, may have been due to the displacement of domestic by Community products in the years immediately following British accession to the EC, just as part of the rise in exports during the same years reflected a like displacement of domestic by British goods in other Community markets. This explanation fits the fall in net imports between 1974 and 1977 shown in chart

2.1. When relative prices turned up after 1976, both gross and net imports rose according to expectations. They failed, however, to respond to the fall in relative United Kingdom prices after 1980, or at least only began to do so in 1985.

There are a number of possible explanations of import behaviour in the 1980s. First, there may be so large a gap between domestic prices and the price of certain imports that the fall in relative United Kingdom prices has had no effect on trade. Low-cost producers in the new industrial and developing countries now have a much larger capacity to produce for export than they did in the mid-1970s, and their absolute price advantage both then and now may be so large that changes in relative prices on the scale of the past ten years have not affected sales. Secondly, goods may be imported because they are not available in the United Kingdom, or not available in sufficient quantity. It is rarely that a product or some close substitute is entirely unavailable but the greater the degree of product differentiation among foreign manufacturers and the greater the desire for variety among consumers, the more important this motive is likely to be; while the loss of capacity in British industry during the recession could have made it physically impossible to satisfy increasing demand. Another, and in some ways related, possibility is that British goods are inferior to foreign products in design and other non-price characteristics. Finally, there is the uncomfortable possibility that the index of relative values we have calculated is wrong, that United Kingdom prices are little if any lower relative to import prices than they were in the early 1980s. These possibilities were discussed with retailers and are explored in the case studies.

IMPORT PENETRATION AND NET IMPORT RATIOS

So far the growth of imports has been compared to demand and output in volume terms. At any more detailed level, short of the individual product, comparisons have to be made in terms of current prices. The share of imports in an industry's domestic market may be calculated by deducting the value of exports from the value of manufacturers' deliveries of characteristic products[2] and adding imports to give an estimate of apparent consumption: apparent consumption equals deliveries *minus* exports *plus* imports; the ratio of imports to apparent consumption is the familiar import penetration ratio, now regularly calculated for most industries by the Department of Trade and Industry. An alternative is to calculate the ratio of imports to total supplies (deliveries *plus* imports equals supplies equals apparent consumption *plus* exports). This has the advantage that a comparable ratio can be calculated for exports and the two may be used to show the balance of trade or net imports

Table 2.4. *Import penetration and net import ratios*

—	Clothing and footwear	Electrical and electronic goods	Other household goods	Other goods	Total
Imports as per cent of apparent consumption[a]					
SIC 1968: 1974	19	30	14	17	19
1979	28	39	18	27	27
SIC 1980: 1979	30	39	18	27	27
1984	37	50	24	40	36
Net imports as per cent of supplies[ab]					
SIC 1968: 1974	7	15	−6	−7	3
1979	10	21	−2	−5	7
SIC 1980: 1979	11	22	−2	−4	7
1984	18	33	7	5	16

Source: See Appendix 1.
[a] Apparent consumption is defined as: output *less* exports *plus* imports. Supplies are defined as output plus imports. No allowance is made for stock changes.
[b] A minus sign indicates net exports.

relative to supplies. This is a better measure of general competitiveness than the import penetration ratio. Clearly if two industries have the same ratio of imports to consumption, but one is a net importer and the other a net exporter, the latter is more competitive in international markets.

Both indicators have two defects. Neither takes account of stock changes so that apparent consumption and supplies may be over or understated in any one year.[3] More seriously, when domestic and trade prices move differently, ratios measured at current prices will give a false reading of the movement of imports in volume terms and so of the effect on output. In some of the case studies where ratios for both the value and volume of certain products can be calculated, changes over time are very different in size and occasionally in direction. As against these deficiencies, however, there is the great advantage of comparing like with like in terms of the goods covered.

Table 2.4 translates the trading experience already described into import penetration and net import ratios for those consumer goods industries with which this study is concerned. The import penetration ratio for the group was initially, in 1974, rather below the average for all manufacturing but by 1979 it was higher and by 1984 very much higher. The average increase was almost the same in both periods (8 and 9 percentage points in 1974–9 and 1979–84 respectively) but this was because of a lower rate of increase in import penetration in clothing and footwear after 1979. Elsewhere import penetration accelerated, especially among 'other goods'. In terms of net imports, British consumer

Table 2.5. *Import penetration and net import ratios for specific industries, 1984*[a]

	Net exporter	Net import ratio			
		10 or less	11–20	21–30	over 30
IP ratio less than 10	Soft furnishings Wallcoverings				
10–19	Toiletries (Soap)		Furniture		
20–29	(China)	Domestic stoves. Women's light outerwear, etc. Domestic metalware			
30–39	Plastic floor coverings	Hats, caps, etc.	Misc. dress Work clothing and jeans Carpets, etc. Hosiery and knitwear Household textiles	Weatherproof outerwear	
40–49			Womens tailored outerwear	Mens shirts. Mens tailored outerwear Domestic electric appliances (Glassware)	Footwear
50–59					
60 and over	Cutlery		Sports goods		Leather goods Gloves Electronic consumer goods Toys and games

Source: Business Monitors, NIESR estimates.
[a] Imports as per cent of home demand, net imports as per cent of supplies. For definitions, see table 2.4.
Note: Brackets indicate rough estimates.

goods industries have long been worse off than manufacturing industry as a whole. As a group they have been net importers throughout the period under review, whereas the United Kingdom has regularly been a net importer of all manufactures only since 1981. In 1984 the trade deficit in relation to supplies was more than two and a half times as large for the consumer goods industries as for all manufacturing.

Table 2.5 shows the two ratios in 1984 for the 29 product groups included in table 2.4. In hardly more than half a dozen instances was the United Kingdom still a net exporter. Generally speaking, net exports tend to be associated with a relatively low level of import penetration and vice versa; but it is perfectly possible to achieve an export surplus even when import penetration is fairly high, as is the case with china and earthenware. (The still more exceptional case of cutlery is somewhat misleading since the data cover both cutlery in the common sense of the word and razors, products with very different trading patterns.) Similarly, there are industries with a very high level of import penetration where net imports are relatively small. But it is broadly true that weakness at home implies weakness abroad.

THE ORIGIN OF IMPORTS

The great bulk of British imports of consumer goods originates in Western Europe and the Far East, and within these areas the predominant suppliers are the European Community and the new industrial countries in Asia – Hong Kong, South Korea, Taiwan and Singapore. Electrical and electronic goods, where Japan outclasses the Community, is the only exception to this pattern among the four major categories of consumer goods.

Table 2.6 shows shares in imports of the same groups of consumer goods as are covered in tables 2.4 and 2.5. Since the data on which table 2.6 is based are classified according to the SITC rather than the SIC, the correspondence is not perfect, but it is sufficiently close to permit direct comparison. The Community, defined as the six original members

Table 2.6. *Shares of major suppliers in United Kingdom imports of consumer goods*

Per cent

		Import shares					Estimated share in UK market
		Clothing and footwear	Electrical and electronic goods	Other household goods	Other goods	Total	
EC[a]	1974	28.9	36.8	44.2	32.5	34.4	7
	1979	33.5	41.8	50.6	40.4	39.6	11
	1984	36.4	35.4	59.6	40.5	41.5	15
EFTA[b]	1974	16.5	19.1	15.9	4.9	16.1	3
	1979	10.0	6.6	11.8	3.6	8.8	2
	1984	9.6	6.6	11.9	3.4	8.5	3
Japan	1974	1.1	28.9	2.6	7.3	9.6	2
	1979	0.4	28.4	1.5	3.7	7.6	2
	1984	0.3	32.5	1.8	4.4	10.0	4
Asian NICs[c]	1974	35.6	7.7	7.5	27.5	22.0	4
	1979	32.2	14.1	7.3	30.5	22.8	6
	1984	29.7	12.8	5.3	32.2	20.8	7
Others	1974	17.9	7.5	29.8	27.8	17.9	3
	1979	23.9	9.1	28.8	21.8	21.2	6
	1984	24.0	12.7	21.4	19.5	19.2	7

Source: OECD Trade Statistics, Eurostat Foreign Trade Statistics, NIESR estimates.
[a] Refers to EC9 throughout.
[b] Including Portugal throughout.
[c] Hong Kong, South Korea, Taiwan and Singapore.

plus Denmark, the Irish Republic and the United Kingdom itself, has steadily increased its share over the past decade, from around one third to more than two fifths of the total. (Taking the Community as at present constituted, that is including Greece, Spain and Portugal, its share in 1984 was 51 per cent of total imports.) Some of its gain, at least from 1974 to 1979, represents the diversion, or rather reversion, of purchases from EFTA as British tariff treatment of goods from the two areas was equalised, but Community gains in the United Kingdom market at the expense of domestic producers were vastly more important. Only in electrical and electronic goods has its share of imports diminished in the face of Japanese competition, and this did not imply a loss of share in the British market because of the rapid increase in total import penetration. This, indeed, is generally true: foreign suppliers may have lost market share to competitors in the import trade but this has rarely implied any significant loss of share in United Kingdom consumption.

The new industrial countries in Asia have experienced some loss of import share, especially in clothing and footwear, and since 1979 in electrical and electronic goods as well. In earlier years at least, most of this was due to the growth of new sources of supply in other, mainly Asian, developing countries. More recently they have lost ground to the Mediterranean associates of the Community, while the rise in United States demand after 1982 may have led to the diversion of supplies there, curtailing sales in the United Kingdom as in the rest of Europe.

No other country, or group of countries, had as much as a 5 per cent share in United Kingdom consumer goods imports in 1984, although they can be very important suppliers of specific products – footwear from Brazil, for example, or glassware and furniture from Eastern Europe. The United States enjoyed a growing share in imports so long as the dollar was weak; as it rose, so trade fell. Other minor suppliers seem to have been elbowed out by the Community, as Britain developed closer ties with its partners.

In the final column of table 2.6, data on import shares have been applied to import penetration ratios for total imports to estimate the share of major foreign suppliers in United Kingdom consumption of manufactured consumer goods. Because of discrepancies in coverage, these figures are inevitably less reliable than those for shares in imports, but there is no reason to suppose that they are seriously inaccurate.

In ten years, the Community rather more than doubled its share of the United Kingdom market, while the rest of the world raised its share by some three quarters. In absolute terms, the Community secured an additional 0.8 per cent of the United Kingdom market both from 1974 to 1979 and from 1979 to 1984. It might have been expected that during the formative years of United Kingdom membership of the Community, its partners would have been gaining market share a good deal more rapidly than other foreign suppliers, and that once tariff abolition had been completed in 1977 or at most within a year or two, the rate at which it gained market share would slacken but there is no sign of that happening as yet. It is true that non-EC countries, which also secured an extra 0.8 per cent of the United Kingdom market annually from 1974 to 1979, have been gaining 1 per cent annually since then, that is rather more than the Community; but their gain was entirely due to the surge in electronic goods which did so much to increase the level of total import penetration. Too much weight should not be given to these figures but they do call in question any simple argument that the rise in import penetration of the United Kingdom market by the rest of the Community was primarily due to British membership of the EC. Certainly in recent years other, and more important, influences were at work.

3

DEVELOPMENTS IN RETAILING

THE STRUCTURE OF RETAILING IN THE UNITED KINGDOM

It is widely believed that British retailing is unique, because of the large scale of operations of major retailers in relation to the size of the market served, and the concentration of the greater part of turnover in the hands of a small number of firms. The large size of the leading retailers gives them substantial market power, a strength that is reinforced by the British consumers' lack of brand-consciousness and the growing importance of own-label products. The market is retailer-led. It was not uncommon in interviews for such remarks to be made as: 'The manufacturer must do as he's told'. Inevitably this has soured relations between manufacturers and retailers, and so undermined one of the potential strengths of the domestic producer – his closeness to his customers. In turn some manufacturers whose bargaining strength is weak relative to major retailers have retaliated on their smaller customers among retailers, thus further souring relations.

Manufacturers complain that the scale of retail business in the United Kingdom has promoted import penetration. Most manufacturers and indeed many retailers regard the market as uniquely open. With substantial buying power concentrated in a few hands and with large retailers importing on their own account, it is easy for foreign suppliers to secure national distribution in this country, whereas the outside supplier in other countries must deal with many more distributors if he is to secure the same result. How far this particular claim is justified lies outside the scope of this survey, but it may be said that a certain amount of evidence was produced in its support. Here, however, we are concerned only with the structure of British retailing and changes in that structure that could have promoted import penetration.

Shares in retailing in 1984 by size of turnover, distinguishing broad kinds of business (KOB) are shown in table 3.1. 150 businesses accounted for 55 per cent of the turnover of retailers other than retailers of food, drink, confectionery, tobacco and newspapers, and repair business. Some of these businesses were very large. Excluding 'other non-food retailers' for which details are not available, 68 businesses had turnover of £50 million or over and seven of these were mixed retailers with turnover of £500 million. In fact these figures understate the role of the large

Table 3.1. *Shares in retailing by size of turnover, including VAT, 1984*

	Clothing, footwear & leather goods	Household goods	Other non-food	Mixed	Total number & value of turnover, £m
Turnover less than £1 million					
No. of retailers	28,181	38,463	34,700	5,101	106,445
% share of total turnover	37.0	41.6	65.2	3.1	12.69
Turnover £1 million – £20 million					
No. of retailers	451	871	635	162	2,119
% share of total turnover	18.3	16.7	24.4	4.1	5.66
Turnover £20 million and over					
No. of retailers	52	45	15	38	150
% share of total turnover	44.7	41.7	10.4	92.8	22.78

Source: Retail Enquiry 1984.
Note: In this and other tables based on the Retail Enquiries, figures relate to Great Britain only and exclude the trade of very small retailers who may number 40,000 but account for less than 1 per cent of all retail turnover. Businesses refer to legal units; some businesses separately recorded in the Enquiries are parts of the same enterprises.

retailer since businesses separately classified for VAT make independent returns, even though they may belong to the same retail enterprise.

Commodity sales according to size of business are classified according to the number of outlets operated by each business, rather than by turnover, and the number of businesses involved is not published. However, the overwhelming majority of single-outlet retailers and small multiples with fewer than ten outlets had turnover of less than £1 million in 1984. Their average turnover in the KOB covered in table 3.1 was £183,000, and it is unlikely that apart from some mixed retailers, mainly department stores, there was any significant number of businesses in this group with turnover of more than £1 million. Data for businesses with fewer than ten outlets may be taken therefore to represent the share of businesses that are also small in terms of turnover for commodity sales.

Table 3.2 shows shares in retailing of commodities grouped as far as possible as in the tables in Chapter 2. Retailers with more than ten outlets had the biggest share in electronic and electrical goods, partly because of the importance of sales by Electricity Board outlets in this sector. They also dominated trade in clothing and footwear. Their share is greatly reduced in other household goods, but still not far short of half. In all other goods their share drops to around two fifths, but the group includes some commodities where big retailers are in a very strong position. These have been distinguished in table 3.2 as 'Other I'. In the remaining group, 'Other II', the large retailers never have more

Table 3.2. *Shares in turnover of retailers classified by numbers of outlets, 1984*

	Total turnover[a] £m	% share of turnover: no. of outlets			
		1	2–9	10–99	over 100
Clothing and footwear	12,736	24.8	14.6	18.9	41.7
Electronic and electrical	6,420	23.0	14.2	14.6	48.2
Other household goods[b]	8,700	33.9	17.8	20.7	27.6
Other I[c]	3,751	19.0	13.4	15.2	51.8
Other II	9,085	47.1	22.8	10.0	20.1
Total	40,692	31.0	16.9	16.3	35.8

Source: Retail Enquiry 1984.
[a] Including VAT.
[b] Carpets, household textiles and soft furnishings, furniture, hardware, china and glass and DIY goods.
[c] Toilet preparations, photographic goods, travel goods and unspecified goods.

than 40 per cent of turnover in any commodity and in some cases less than 30 per cent. Other II covers products largely falling outside the scope of this study; the most important in terms of turnover are drugs, stationery and books, and jewellery.

CHANGES IN STRUCTURE: THE INDEPENDENT RETAILER

For many years past and more particularly since the last war, the share of multiple retailers in turnover has been increasing. Between 1950 and 1970 it roughly doubled, with food multiples increasing their share still faster. The abolition of resale price maintenance created new opportunities for the multiples and contributed to the 'pile it high sell it cheap' style of retailing that was such a feature of the 1970s. There has been a corresponding decline in the share of small, single-outlet retailers and the small multiples that are unable to compete with the multiples on price or to exploit the new techniques that the multiples have deployed to increase centralised control and cut costs. The more traditional types of retailing (cooperatives and department stores as well as independent specialists) are under strong competitive pressure. The biggest changes so far have been in food retailing with the development of supermarkets and then superstores, and the construction of stores on the edge or out of town to serve customers who cannot find parking space in town centres. In non-food retailing it has until now been chiefly the very big retailers of household goods that have followed food retailers out of town, but other firms are beginning to move too. At the same time, wherever their outlets are located, the big retailers are adopting new technology that allows centralised warehousing and distribution and sophisticated electronic accounting and stock control. These changes are clearly going

Table 3.3. *Single outlet and small multiple retailers: change in numbers and share of turnover including VAT*

Kind of business	1976–8[a]	1978–80	1980–2	1982–4	Actual 1984
Clothing, footwear and leather goods					
No. of businesses, 000s	−6.1	−2.0	−2.7	−0.2	28.5
Share of group turnover, %	−1.5	−0.7	−2.3	−1.6	45.2
Household goods retailers					
No. of businesses, 000s	−2.0	−0.5	−1.8	+0.3	39.3
Share of group turnover, %	−1.0	−0.5	−0.8	−6.0	55.0
Other specialist retailers					
No. of businesses, 000s	−3.3	+1.6	+0.2	+1.6	35.2
Share of group turnover, %	−1.2	+0.4	−0.4	+1.6	82.8
Mixed retail business					
No. of businesses, 000s	...	−0.1	+1.7	+0.1	5.3
Share of group turnover, %	...	−0.5	−5.2	+0.1	27.9
Total					
No. of businesses, 000s	...	−1.1	−2.5	+1.8	108.2
Share of total turnover, %	...	+0.2	−2.3	−1.4	48.1
of which:					
small multiples with 2–9 outlets					
No. of businesses, 000s	...	+2.0	−0.9	+0.4	17.6
Share of total turnover, %	...	−0.7	−1.0	−0.4	17.0

Source: Retail Enquiries, various.
[a] Based on previous KOB classification which is not comparable to that currently in use.

to go much further. The widespread introduction of electronic point of sale systems (EPOS), linked into a national funds transfer network, could be the most revolutionary change of all. Meanwhile the large retailers that have not already done so are hastening to introduce their own charge and credit cards and a variety of services to encourage the public to deal with them, rather than their smaller competitors.

What has happened is modest by comparison with what is likely to come. Between 1976, when the first Retail Enquiry of the current type was undertaken, and 1984, the fall in numbers and in the share of turnover of small retailers seems to have been fairly gradual. Unfortunately, because of changes in methods of calculating numbers of small retailers and in the KOB classification, it is not possible to obtain a straight run of figures. Instead, changes between years for which data comparable in classification and coverage are available must be used. This is done in table 3.3 for the four broad KOB categories. It should be noted that because of the trade of mixed retailers, the loss to small retailers in the specialist categories is not equal to the loss of small firms in terms of the commodities typically sold by such kinds of business. Specialists in clothing and related products conduct little more than half the trade in these goods, specialists in household goods about two thirds of trade, other specialists less than 60 per cent of the trade in their specialities.

From table 3.3 it appears that the net loss of small non-food businesses in terms of numbers since 1978 has been comparatively small, of the order of 2,000 at most, although the rate of loss may have been higher in earlier years. The fall in the number of clothing and household goods retailers has been offset by a rise in other specialist and mixed retailers; while since 1982 there has been a rise, or as in clothing a slower rate of decline. Loss of market share in terms of turnover has been well under 5 per cent in total since 1978 but it persisted after 1982, being particularly severe in the case of household goods retailers. Relative to their share of trade, small multiples appear to have experienced a greater loss of market share than single outlet retailers, although this could be the result of successful small multiples moving up into the ranks of larger businesses, rather than being squeezed out by their bigger competitors.[1]

THE GROWTH OF LARGE FIRMS

The converse of the small retailers' declining share of turnover is a rising share for the large multiple retailers, but this rise has not been matched by an increase in the number of businesses. The number of multiple retailers with ten or more outlets fell by over 100 between 1978 and 1984, and was probably falling at least as rapidly in earlier years. By 1984, there were 528 businesses in this group with average turnover in excess of £40 million. Because, as already noted, component parts of large firms may make separate returns in the Retail Enquiry, these figures seriously overstate the number of very large firms actually engaged in retailing. In order to provide a better guide to their importance we have assembled data, based primarily on company reports, showing turnover of the 50 largest non-food retailers in the United Kingdom, other than retailers that are part of major manufacturing groups such as the footwear shops owned by Clarks. It has to be admitted that these figures too are imperfect. In principle they relate to United Kingdom retail turnover only, exclusive of VAT; in practice some overseas and/or non-retail business may be included and it has been necessary to estimate a good many figures, while among the smaller retailers listed some firms may have been wrongly included, and others thereby excluded.[2] We believe, however, that the data are sufficiently reliable to be useful; their very deficiencies may encourage the publication of fuller information in future.

The findings are summarised in table 3.4 where they are compared with the total turnover of non-food retailers, including turnover derived

Table 3.4. *Shares of major retail enterprises in turnover of non-food retailers: selected years*

Per cent of total turnover excluding VAT	1976	1980	1984
5 largest	22.8	22.5	24.8
10 largest	33.4	33.0	35.4
20 largest	42.2	42.5	46.1
50 largest	48.5	50.6	54.3
Total turnover of non-food retailers excluding VAT, £m	15,493[a]	26,294	36,713

Source: Appendix 2, Retail Enquiries.
[a] Estimated.

from food sales by mixed retailers. Two points stand out. First, the 50 largest retail enterprises account for more than half of all retail turnover of non-food shops, five accounting for one quarter of the total in 1984. Secondly, the shares of the top five, the top ten and the top twenty barely changed between 1976 and 1980; but by 1984 signs of change are emerging with major retailers' share of turnover rising and more new names coming into the list – changes that have been carried further in the past two years.

Part of the stability reflects the sheer size of the six or seven largest retailers relative to their competitors, and especially the dominant position of Marks and Spencer. Even ignoring its very large sales of food, around two fifths of United Kingdom turnover in the financial year equivalent to 1984, it is still the largest single non-food retailer in the country; the combined turnover of the three businesses grouped in Woolworths Holdings, ranking second to Marks and Spencer in 1984, was approximately equal to the latter's non-food turnover in that year but still not much over half the size of its total turnover. Marks and Spencer has raised its share of non-food retailers' turnover from under 7 to almost 9 per cent in the period covered by table 3.3, thus accounting for almost the whole of the top five's increase in share between 1976 and 1984.

Immediately below Marks and Spencer in the ranking, there has been some jostling for position between GUS, Sears, Woolworths, Boots and Littlewoods, but collectively they have retained the next five places after Marks and Spencer throughout. All these firms span more than one KOB; though with the possible exception of Sears with its very large interest in footwear retailing through the British Shoe Corporation, and to some extent Boots, the core of their business is some form of mixed retailing. Boots itself is classed in the Retail Enquiry as a mixed retailer, despite popular perception of it as a specialist and its very strong position in sales of chemists goods.

The comparative stability in the ranking and the bias towards mixed retailing (department and variety stores and mail order houses) continued through the rest of the top twenty from 1976 to 1980. Only Burton and Empire Stores dropped out, to be replaced by MFI and Comet which raised the number of specialist retailers in the top twenty from five to six, the others being C. & A. Modes,[3] the Electricity Council, Curry's, and the British Gas Corporation. By 1984, however, two firms had hoisted themselves into the top ten (Dixons, thanks to its takeover of Curry's, and W. H. Smith) and three into the top twenty (Burton making a comeback, Harris Queensway, and Argos).

These three and Dixons are among the retailing 'high fliers' that achieved an improvement in their ranking of at least ten places from 1976 to 1984 or of five places in either of the two sub-periods. Other high fliers were: Comet until its takeover by Woolworths Holdings; Fine Art Developments (probably); Habitat/Mothercare, like Dixons an inherently vigorous retailer that moved sharply up the ranking following its merger with another and larger enterprise; Home Charm; MFI; Next, formerly Hepworths; and four newcomers – Homebase, Lasky's, Superdrug and Ward White.

THE 'NEW' RETAILERS

The high fliers developed their business both by organic growth, the expansion of existing businesses, and by acquisition. Harris Queensway is the outstanding example of the latter process. Since 1977 when the then Harris Carpets Ltd purchased 25 Queensway Discount Warehouses, roughly doubling its turnover, hardly a year has passed without a major acquisition: Ross & Company in 1978, Hardy & Company in 1979, Henderson Kenton and a discount business that became Poundstretcher in 1980, twelve New Day Furnishing Stores and ten U Kay Furnishing centres in 1981, General George Carpets in 1982 and Bakers Household Stores in 1984. It raised the number of its outlets over the same period from 93 to 680. Others have been less acquisitive but several of them made important purchases as they grew. Burton acquired 223 Dorothy Perkins shops in 1979, raising the number of its outlets by a third; Dixons acquired 22 Greens photographic and hi-fi stores from Debenhams in 1979, but it has generally preferred to develop its own new sites. Less rapidly-growing retailers too have made acquisitions. What distinguished the high fliers from the rest was that they were all prepared to invest heavily, to refurbish and modernise existing stores, to centralise buying and stockholding, and to market aggressively.

Other than this, it is not easy to discern a common pattern in their growth but most of them share one or more of the following characteristics. They are specialist firms operating in rapidly growing markets such as DIY and electronic consumer goods, for example Home Charm and Dixons. They are specialist firms with a carefully structured approach in slower growing markets, involving precise market segmentation and often a strong design element both in the goods sold and in the actual business of retailing. The transformation of a conservative clothing retailer, Hepworths, into Next is the supreme example and the most influential in terms of its impact on other retailers, but elements of a similar approach are to be found among other high fliers, notably of course Habitat and the revitalised Burton. Their approach may be summed up in terms of the statement in Burton's 1985 Annual Report that: 'Market stratification, not by socio-economic class alone, but by consumer preferences and lifestyles, is fundamental to the Group's approach to the market place'. In similar vein, Dixons' Annual Report stated: 'Competitive advantage is gained by establishing and maintaining superior ranges of products ... Marketing should stimulate demand for proven products and create demand for new ones'. Finally, there are the firms that have concentrated on beating the competition by keeping down prices, particularly in the sales of electrical and household goods but including also Argos, a catalogue retailer, and Superdrug, so far the biggest and most successful of the new drugstores, which deals in toiletries, health foods and household goods. Apart from these two last firms and Ward White, the high fliers are also essentially specialist retailers. It is perhaps this emphasis on specialised retailing (allowing that specialisation may take different forms) which marks developments in the late 1970s and early 1980s, though whether it will persist is another matter. Some of the specialists – Next is again an example – are already moving into market sectors removed from their core business.

Since 1984, a number of mergers and takeovers have carried the changes so far described a good deal further. They include: the takeover of Foster Brothers Clothing as well as a number of smaller clothing and related chains by Sears, and of Debenhams by Burton; the merger of Habitat/Mothercare with British Home Stores to form Storehouse, of MFI and ADG, and of Next and Grattan; the takeover of Home Charm by Ladbroke, Lasky's parent; the acquisition of Superdrug by Woolworths; and Ward White's buying spree in the course of which it has acquired Owen Owen, Payless, Halfords and Zodiac, thereby probably boosting its turnover to something over £400 million. There have also been some acquisitions that have had less marked effects on total turnover but that are nevertheless important because they have given the purchaser a commanding position in a particular sector of the retail market, for example Smith's purchase of Our Price which raised its share of recorded music sales from 12 to 18 per cent; and the takeover by

Ratners, a high-flier previously not in the top fifty, of H. Samuel, the big multiple jeweller. One other move should be noted: the purchase of Times Furnishing and Thoms from GUS by Harris Queensway and the close association that appears to be developing between the two parties to the transaction. In almost all these cases, it is one of the high fliers that has taken the initiative.

Sufficient information is not yet available to update the figures in table 3.4 and Appendix 2 to illustrate the consequences of these moves, but some idea of the effects on market share may be obtained by adding together recent data on turnover of formerly separate groups that are now part of the same organisation. The results are, of course, artificial in that they make no allowance for the effect of sales of shops acquired during takeovers and subsequently sold because they do not fit into the new owner's pattern of trading. More importantly, they ignore the possibility that the assets acquired will be more vigorously exploited than was likely under their previous ownership. It appears, for example, that Dixons increased sales from Curry's in 1985 more rapidly than the previous owners had been able to do in the preceding two years. It seems probable, however, that mergers or takeovers have promoted two newcomers, Burton and Storehouse, with 1984 equivalent turnover of more than £1 billion and £850 million respectively, to the top ten. (Debenhams was already there before it was acquired by Burton.) Two others, Ward White and Next/Grattan, with 1984 equivalent turnover of £405 million and £340 million, will move into the top twenty, while the hand of such energetic retailers as Harris Queensway and MFI will be further strengthened. Harris Queensway's 1984 turnover would have exceeded £500 million if its purchases from GUS had been in effect then; the furniture and carpet turnover of MFI/ADG would have exceeded £400 million. At a minimum, the share of the top ten in total non-food retailers' turnover will rise by some $1\frac{1}{2}$ per cent, of the top twenty by around 2. In fact it is probable that twenty retail enterprises will very shortly conduct more than half the total turnover of non-food retailers, if indeed they do not already do so; and this is the more likely since the new entrants are stimulating competitive changes in retailing styles and methods among the old-established leaders, notably Marks and Spencer, inducing a more carefully targeted, more aggressive approach on their part also.

SECTORAL MARKET SHARES AND CONCENTRATION

The growth of large, new retail enterprises is having a significant effect on market share in certain sectors of retailing. Specialist DIY retailing provides the most striking example. As recently as 1980, the top three, Home Charm, B. & Q. and A. G. Stanley, accounted for 15.6 per cent

of the turnover of DIY specialists. By 1984, with A. G. Stanley replaced
by Payless, they accounted for 36.4 per cent, while the top five had
45 per cent of turnover. The share of the top five furniture and carpet
retailers is uncertain because separate figures for sales by GUS subsidiaries are not available, but Harris Queensway and MFI had together
about 3 per cent of turnover in 1976, almost 12 per cent in 1980 and
over 20 per cent in 1984. Taking later mergers and acquisitions into
account brings their combined share to over one quarter. Concentration
among leading specialists in the electrical/musical group has long been
relatively high; over a quarter for the top three in 1976 and approaching
one third in 1980. By then the top five had close on 35 per cent of
sales and following Curry's takeover of Dixons their share rose to around
40 per cent.

This still leaves concentration among specialist KOB way below that
in mixed retailing. The Monopolies and Mergers Commission estimated
that in 1981 five firms accounted for well over 90 per cent of mail order
turnover,[4] and there is no reason to suppose that the situation has changed
significantly. A recent market research report put their share at 97 per
cent: GUS, the market leader, is credited with more than 40 per cent.
In mixed retailing other than mail order, the share of the five leading
variety stores rose from something under 60 per cent in 1976 to close
on two thirds in 1984.

Official retail concentration data were first published in the 1982
Enquiry and repeated, on a changed classification, in 1984. The results
are shown in table 3.5. It should be noted that these figures refer to
businesses in common ownership, that is enterprises, unlike any of the
other data in the Retail Enquiries. Sales are classified in terms of
commodity groups rather than KOB. The results imply that seller concentration is on the low side, reaching a maximum for the five largest
enterprises of 44 per cent in footwear where the British Shoe Corporation
alone holds more than a quarter of the market. It is more commonly
less than a third for the top five and less than a half for the top ten.
In most cases where figures for both 1982 and 1984 are available concentration has risen, especially in DIY and decorators' supplies, furniture
and carpets, with the whole of the rise accruing to the top five. The
shares of the next largest firms have tended to diminish.

It is debatable whether these figures really give an adequate indication
of seller concentration in retailing. Some of the categories are very widely
drawn and even within more precisely defined categories retailers may
concentrate on specific products or market sectors, implying a significantly higher degree of concentration. Marks and Spencer is generally
reckoned to have around 15 per cent of the total clothing market by
value, but its share in the middle market sector where it operates and

Table 3.5. *Concentration in sales of major non-food consumer goods, 1982 and 1984*

| | Per cent of total sales including VAT by: | | | |
| | Largest 5 enterprises | | Largest 10 enterprises | |
	1982	1984	1982	1984
Footwear	43.3	44.4	52.8	53.3
Toilet preparations, cosmetics, etc.	...	42.5	...	56.1
Domestic appliances, lawn mowers	...	42.4	...	55.7
Photographic and optical goods	38.8	41.9	48.9	51.6
Men's and boy's wear	33.4	35.7	44.1	45.7
Furniture, floor coverings, etc.*a*	25.8	32.2	36.5	41.4
Women's, girls', children's and infants' wear	32.1	30.7	43.7	42.9
Travel goods, handbags, etc.	29.5	28.9	45.7	43.2
Carpets, carpeting and rugs	23.4	28.6	31.4	34.6
DIY and decorators' supplies	21.7	28.0	35.3	39.5
Lighting and minor electrical	...	26.9	...	36.4
Audio/visual equipment, home computers, musical instruments, etc.	...	25.8	...	37.3
Household textiles and soft furnishings	24.0	24.9	34.5	37.2
Hardware, china, glassware and cutlery	24.1	23.8	32.9	34.4
Jewellery, silverware, watches and clocks	18.0	20.4	26.6	30.2
Sports goods, toys, games and camping equipment*b*	18.1	17.5	26.6	25.0

Source: Retail Enquiries.
a Perambulators and prints included in 1984 but excluded in 1982.
b Cycles included in 1984 and perambulators excluded. The latter were included in 1982.

in certain product lines is significantly higher. In shirts, for example, it claims to purchase about half of total United Kingdom output of woven shirts which would give it something of the order of 30 per cent of United Kingdom sales by value, though less by volume. This is a special case, but it does illustrate the possibility that concentration at the product level, which is what concerns the manufacturer, can be very much higher than broadly-based data indicate.

Because of the protean character of retailing and the segmentation of the market in a variety of ways – by style, by class and income, by geography – it is hard to envisage a classification that would give a fair picture of retail concentration. Some markets are becoming narrower as retailers target ever more precisely. Others merge and overlap. Shops specialising in furniture or carpets or household furnishings are giving way to enterprises that embrace all three, and more besides. The DIY chains are moving into their territory, selling fitted kitchens and electrical goods. Sports shops sell clothes; childrenswear shops sell toys and baby goods. The big retailers are developing this approach with, for example,

Boots launching Children's World and Marks and Spencer developing satellite stores catering to particular groups of consumers.

However markets are defined it is doubtful that concentration as such is a problem, with perhaps a few exceptions, and it is clear that retailing is very competitive. What does matter is the discrepancy in size between the large or very large retailer and the, often small, manufacturer. Many of the rapidly-growing retailers follow Marks and Spencer's practice of working closely with their suppliers, which can ameliorate industry's difficulties but does not resolve them. An efficient firm with a turnover exceeding £1 billion and commensurate buying power must be in a stronger position than a manufacturer whose turnover is less than a tenth or a twentieth as large. This problem is explored further in the case studies where we attempt to illustrate the discrepancy in size between retailers and manufacturers in specific industries, and its consequences.

WHO BUYS IMPORTS?

Another point explored more fully in the case studies is the question of who actually handles imports from overseas: retailer, import merchant or manufacturer? There seems to be a tendency in some quarters to assume that because large retailers import direct, their activities alone explain import penetration. There are two points at issue: do large retailers buy abroad very extensively, as opposed to acquiring imports through other channels, and are they exceptionally dependent on imports? A summary answer to these questions is provided here, based on questionnaires and interviews relating to reasons for importing that are discussed in the next chapter. Replies confirmed that large retailers are indeed heavily engaged in direct importing. Almost three quarters of a sample of over 100 retailers and retail buyers reported that imported goods were purchased directly overseas or through import agents and associated companies. Rather more than half the sample purchased imported goods from United Kingdom manufacturers who were importing on their own account, two fifths used import merchants, and fewer than 15 per cent purchased imports from wholesalers. Outside the clothing and footwear trades, however, it was rare for a retailer to rely exclusively on direct importing, and even here only one in three did so. This was one of several differences between trade in clothing and footwear and in other goods; others were an above-average degree of direct importing (over 90 per cent), more widespread use of wholesalers, from whom about one in five purchased some imports, and rather more limited use of import merchants than was the general rule. Among retailers of electrical and electronic goods, imports were chiefly purchased from manufacturer-importers. Only one in three retailers imported directly and limited use was made of wholesalers. (Because of the small size and unrepresentative character of this part of the sample, these figures may be misleading.) Finally, two thirds of retailers of other, mainly household, goods imported directly, almost 60 per cent used import merchants, just under half secured imports via manufacturers and fewer than 10 per cent used wholesalers.

Small retailers were asked not how they obtained imports but how they obtained all goods whatever their origin. Out of a sample of more than 200 retailers, 95 per cent dealt directly with United Kingdom manufacturers and more than 80 per cent with foreign manufacturers and their representatives. In addition, two thirds of the sample used wholesalers and about one third dealt with importers. Almost one in three made some purchases through retail buying groups, but very few (less than 10 per cent) resorted to cash-and-carry wholesalers. Again there were marked differences in the pattern between groups. All specialist clothing retailers dealt directly with United Kingdom manufacturers, almost 80 per cent with foreign manufacturers, over half with importers and two fifths with wholesalers. Group purchasing was not important with only about one in ten using this method but almost a quarter used cash-and-carry wholesalers. A slightly smaller proportion (90 per cent) of retailers of electronic and electrical goods dealt with manufacturers operating in the United Kingdom, a much higher proportion with wholesalers (70 per cent) and group wholesalers (33 per cent). Contact with foreign manufacturers was about average but comparatively few dealt directly with importers and there was little or no use made of cash-and-carry wholesalers. Among the remainder, mixed retailers and dealers in household goods, contacts with United Kingdom and foreign manufacturers were close to the average for all small retailers but extensive use was made of wholesalers (by 72 per cent), importers (64 per cent) and group wholesalers (38 per cent) while dependence on cash-and-carry was rather above average, though this may simply reflect the fact that many of the firms concerned sold clothing along with other products.

Two comments may be made on these figures. First, they confirm the virtual disappearance of wholesaling to large retailers outside clothing and electronic/electrical goods; and they show that, although small retailers continue to make extensive use of wholesalers, they do so very much less than in the late 1960s and early 1970s when more than 90 per cent of their purchases may have come from wholesalers. Secondly, there is nothing in the replies by small retailers to suggest that imports now form a lower proportion of their sales than they do of those of the larger retailers, whatever may have been the case in the past. The actual proportion of imports in sales is unknown, but the purchasing methods used suggest that it is often very high.

4

THE BUYER'S POINT OF VIEW

A major part of the research programme was directed to eliciting retailers' replies to two questions: what is the importance of various factors in purchasing decisions; and how do British goods and manufacturers rate against overseas competitors in respect of these factors? This was done by means of questionnaires sent to retailers either directly or through the good offices of the National Chamber of Trade. The bulk of the questionnaires was posted and returned during the summer and autumn of 1986. In addition, retailers interviewed were asked to complete the questionnaires besides providing more precise and detailed information in discussion. The large specialist retailers were asked to complete questionnaires with reference to their main line of business: clothing, footwear and so forth. Large mixed retailers were asked to fill in separate questionnaires for different products or product lines. Small retailers approached indirectly were asked to indicate what types of products they sold. In interviews, respondents were asked to reply in relation to specific products, and their replies are considered more fully in the case studies that follow. Here we simply summarise retailers' broad views on different categories of goods. Copies of the different questionnaires, which included certain additional questions for different groups of retailers, will be found in Appendix 3.

PURCHASING FACTORS

It was by no means easy to select the points for inclusion in the questionnaires. The list of factors that might be taken into account in deciding to buy is very long, and each major point could be broken down into a series of sub-points. Price, for example, is not simply a matter of a specific price for a specific product, but also involves credit and payment terms, quantity discounts and so on. However, in order to elicit a response it was obviously necessary to keep the questionnaires short; so only factors that might be of importance to most retailers could be included, and they had to be baldly and briefly presented without qualification or subdivision. Further, it was thought desirable to keep the same list of factors for all products in order to permit comparisons across different categories of goods, despite the fact that some considerations that are very important in purchasing, say, a technically-complex piece of electronic equipment, may be of no importance to buyers of fashion clothing or of giftware and vice versa.

It was, of course, clear from the start that price was one of the purchasing factors that must be included but the choice and definition of non-price factors was more problematic. Much has been said and written on the importance of design and of what might be called services by manufacturers, but too often such statements are merely vague exhortations to improvement in these matters. Marketing literature is more precise and more useful; but the most helpful guidance was found in the publications of the Design Council and NEDO, and in the statements of retailers themselves, particularly in the memorandum submitted by the Retail Consortium to the House of Commons Industry and Trade Committee and in the Consortium's replies to the Committee's questions.[1] It was said there that the main factors leading to the purchase of foreign rather than British goods were: price; delivery; quality (notably the better finish of goods imported from high-cost countries); the availability of more comprehensive product ranges overseas and greater capacity to produce in volume; overseas suppliers' more immediate response to enquiries and their greater responsiveness to design requirements; and finally the inadequacy of United Kingdom industry's investment in production facilities. These comments related mainly to clothing but similar points were made about other goods: footwear, consumer electronics, furniture. The retailers' attitude may be summed up in the complaint that British manufacturers are still production-oriented rather than market-oriented. This is a comment that can be found over and over again in the literature and was often made in interviews, and not interviews with retailers alone.

Guided by these studies, a list was drawn up of ten factors that might be of major importance in making decisions to purchase:

1. Price
2. Style and appearance
3. Quality of materials and workmanship
4. Product performance
5. Novelty/technological innovation
6. Speed and reliability of delivery
7. Advertising and promotion by supplier
8. Close and frequent contact with supplier
9. Supplier's knowledge of the market
10. Flexibility of supply.

Numbers 2 to 5 are essentially design factors; numbers 6 to 10 relate to the service provided by suppliers. To cater for serious omissions, respondents were asked to specify any additional factors that were considered important, but surprisingly few did so. Happily, still fewer of those who responded questioned the relevance of the factors listed. The response rate to the questionnaires sent out by post was, on average, close to 50 per cent and in only one instance did a retailer indicate that, in his view, the wrong questions were being asked.

In the first question, retailers were asked to indicate whether each factor is: very important, important, of some importance, or does not matter in making purchasing decisions. In the second question, retailers were asked whether they rated British products and producers better, about the same, or worse than foreign products and producers in respect of the same factors. (In the case of price it was indicated that British products were to be rated better if their price was lower and vice versa.)[2] Obviously this was not a matter where judgement could be very precise. The merits and demerits of British and foreign products may well differ from item to item within a given class. A certain type of tableware, for example, may be cheaper abroad than in Britain and another type cheaper in Britain. Or again, within a given product group, what is produced in the United Kingdom may be so different in character from goods imported that comparisons are impossible. Most respondents took these problems in their stride; some distinguished between different items within a group in their replies; others added the comment that they could give only rough answers which were by no means true over the whole range of goods within a group; while still others threw in their hands and omitted certain points or ignored the question completely. The more various the range of goods purchased by the respondent, the harder obviously it was to reply. Even among respondents interviewed where answers could be related to specific products, a certain lack of precision was unavoidable.

It should be emphasised, therefore, that the replies to the questionnaires can only be treated as approximations, as broad indicators of generally perceived differences. There is probably no instance where a respondent would not, if given the opportunity, qualify his or her replies and distinguish exceptions to their general estimate of British and foreign goods and suppliers. In favour of our approach, however, it is only fair to point out that the replies to questionnaires were, with very few exceptions, internally consistent; that it was obvious from many of the comments that the respondents had thought carefully about their answers; and that, since retailers are busy people, the response rate would have been lower if the enquiry had been deemed pointless.

The replies are summarised in tabular form in the sections that follow. The purchasing factors are listed in abbreviated form in the first column of each table. The next two columns show the number of respondents against each heading in question 1 and the percentage score for each factor. In a number of cases, respondents did not mark all the factors listed. On occasion they wrote in not applicable or some similar comment against one or more. In question 1 this was treated as being equivalent to 'Does not matter'. The percentage score for each factor was calculated by allotting 3 points if the purchasing factor in question was marked very important, 2 points for important, 1 for some importance and 0 for does not matter, totalling the points and calculating their ratio to the maximum possible score. If all respondents indicated that price was very important it would score 100 per cent; if all indicated that it was important it would score 67 per cent, and so on. The percentages thus indicate the average degree of importance attached to each factor by all respondents.

The remaining columns cover replies to question 2. Column 4 gives the number of replies. It will be noticed that in many cases the number of replies for a factor in question 2 was low when its score was low in question 1, since many respondents who indicated in question 1 that it did not matter did not mark it in question 2. The next three columns record the number of times that British goods were said to be better, about the same or worse than foreign supplies. Where a respondent indicated that British goods were better in part of the group, say, menswear, and worse in, say, womenswear, this was counted as a half mark for better and a half for worse. The final 'weighted balance' column shows the excess or shortfall of 'better' over 'worse' weighted by the importance given by the respondent to that factor. If retailer A considered price very important and British prices were higher than foreign the reply was scored −3, if retailer B thought that price was important but British prices lower, his score was +2; the weighted sum for the two retailers would then be −1. The weighted balance thus gives a clearer idea of how important the strengths and weaknesses of British suppliers are.

Certain additional questions were put to both large and small retailers. Those relating to methods of purchase are described elsewhere, in Chapter 3 and in the case studies. Here, however, we shall also summarise the replies given by large retailers who answered postal questionnaires and by firms interviewed on the share of imports in purchases, the origin of imports, the age and class of their customers, and their reasons for importing.

Respondents were asked to indicate whether imports constituted less than 10 per cent, 10 to 25 per cent, over 25 to 40 per cent, or over 40 per cent of purchases for resale. Less than 10 per cent is of course a very low proportion, over 40 per cent very high and the two intermediate groups rather below and above the average share of imports in total

United Kingdom consumption of consumer goods. Areas of purchase
to be indicated were Western Europe, Eastern Europe and the USSR,
the United States, Japan, other Far Eastern and Asian countries, Latin
America, Africa and the rest of the world. Age groups were under 25,
25 to 40, over 40 years, and all ages. Classes were A and B, C, D and
E, and again all. The object of these questions was to discover if there
was any obvious bias in the sample with certain categories of business
over- or under-represented. That retailers were asked why they imported
does not need explaining: their replies are discussed at the end of this
chapter and in the case studies. These questions were not included in
the questionnaires sent to small retailers, since it appeared unlikely that
they would be able to give comprehensive replies.

CLOTHING, FOOTWEAR AND RELATED PRODUCTS

Table 4.1 summarises replies to the questionnaire from sixteen specialist
multiple clothing retailers, twelve multiple footwear retailers and from
twenty-one questionnaires relating to specific items of clothing, including
a number completed by the clothing departments of mixed retailers.
The share of imports in purchases ranged from less than 10 to over
40 per cent among clothing retailers but, with one exception, was 25
to 40 per cent or over 40 per cent for footwear retailers. Most firms
imported from Western Europe, the Far East or both; a few also bought
from Eastern Europe; some of the footwear retailers bought from Brazil;
and one or two firms made purchases elsewhere. In terms of import-
dependence and the origin of imports the sample appears to have been
fairly comprehensive. Footwear retailers replying operated in all sectors
of the market but replies relating to clothing were rather heavily slanted
towards the middle and upper income groups; retailers catering specifically to the less well-to-do were under-represented, which may have
affected the scoring of purchasing factors.

As table 4.1 shows, price is not the most important determinant of
purchases. Style and appearance achieved the highest score, followed
by quality of materials and workmanship, delivery and performance.
Price ranked fifth, followed by flexibility of supply and close and frequent
contact with suppliers. Suppliers' knowledge of the market also carried
weight but novelty and supplier promotion, particularly the latter, were
generally considered of little or no importance. Style and appearance
were rated very important by every single specialist retailer of clothing
though not by all footwear and mixed retailers; even so they achieved
the highest average score for footwear retailers too. The big mixed
retailers laid greater emphasis on quality. Both the larger specialist
clothing shops and the mixed retailers, especially the former group,

Table 4.1. *Analysis of replies to questionnaire by large firms retailing clothing and footwear*

| | Importance of purchasing factors | | Compared with foreign supplies British goods are: | | | | |
	No. of replies	% score	No. of replies	Better	About the same	Worse	Weighted balance
Price	49	76	49	$3\frac{1}{2}$	$13\frac{1}{2}$	32	$-69\frac{1}{4}$
Style	48	94	50	$5\frac{1}{4}$	$24\frac{1}{3}$	$20\frac{2}{3}$	$-48\frac{2}{3}$
Quality	49	85	50	$5\frac{1}{2}$	28	$16\frac{1}{2}$	$-31\frac{1}{2}$
Performance	49	82	50	7	38	5	$+7$
Novelty	49	33	44	$10\frac{1}{2}$	$16\frac{1}{2}$	17	$-17\frac{1}{2}$
Delivery	49	84	50	$20\frac{1}{2}$	20	$9\frac{1}{2}$	$+37$
Promotion	47	19	42	22	16	4	$+18$
Contact	49	63	50	32	18	0	$+63$
Knowledge	47	60	49	27	19	3	$+41$
Flexibility	47	65	49	25	14	10	$+32$

stressed the importance of speedy and reliable delivery, which ranked equal with style in the first case and with quality in the second. Footwear retailers were more concerned with product performance and rated price third in the ranking of purchasing factors. The remaining factors had identical ranking across all four sub-groups, although the big specialist clothing retailers laid exceptional emphasis on close contact with suppliers while the mixed retailers gave knowledge of the market a high score. The pre-eminence of style and appearance in purchasing decisions is apparent, with four out of five retailers in the group as a whole marking it 'very important'. Between one half and two thirds of respondents marked quality, performance and delivery very important, two out of five price and less than a quarter of all replies rated contact, knowledge and flexibility of supply very important.

When it comes to a comparison between British and foreign goods and suppliers, the home team is rated almost as badly on style and appearance as on price and also comes out badly on quality, where clothing retailers in particular thought poorly of British goods. The weighted balance for novelty/technology is a sizeable negative, given the small importance attached to this factor. The home team is superior in maintaining close and frequent contact, in knowledge of the market and in delivery, flexibility of supply and promotion as well as, by a small margin, in product performance where the weighted balance was positive for footwear. In all except the last the domestic manufacturer should have an inbuilt advantage over foreign suppliers and it is evidence of continuing slackness in setting and meeting delivery dates that as many as ten respondents, nine of them retailers of clothing, should find British manufacturers worse than their competitors in this respect.

The fractions in table 4.1 generally reflect replies where the retailer's judgement varied according to specific products; but one respondent split his reply on price because he found British prices lower than those of Western Europe but higher than those of the Far East, another found that the quality of British workmanship was better but of materials about the same, and a third found United Kingdom delivery faster but less reliable. There were few other comments, though some respondents indicated that suppliers' ability to produce special products could be a factor. The low rating given to promotion by suppliers was explained by the fact that most of the retailers concerned promoted their own name and the promotion of manufacturers' brands was irrelevant.

Table 4.2 analyses replies from 75 small retailers of clothing and related products. The great majority were single outlet retailers; but thirteen had two to nine outlets, putting them in the small multiples category and one had ten or more outlets. There were 28 specialist clothing retailers of whom seventeen dealt in womenswear only, 29 firms dealing principally in clothing but also selling footwear, household textiles and occasionally other household goods, leisure goods, toys and the like (the old-fashioned drapers), four that were primarily retailers of footwear and 28 which, although they too all sold clothing, would probably be classed as mixed retailers. There was also one drapers which made separate returns for each department. Their replies are not included in table 4.2 but are discussed later.

Once again style and appearance had the highest score of any purchasing factor, though it was of less outstanding importance than among the larger clothing retailers and the non-specialist clothing firms ranked quality marginally higher. This was one of only two instances in which the ranking of factors differed between sub-groups; the other was that small mixed retailers rated product performance second to and almost as highly as style and appearance, possibly because of the importance of household equipment and other durables in their sales. Otherwise the ranking of factors was identical as between clothing specialists, drapers and mixed retailers. For the group as a whole the ranking was very similar to that for the large clothing and footwear retailers, with price once again ranking fifth after style and appearance, quality, performance and delivery. However, more weight was given by small than by large retailers to promotion, reflecting the small retailer's greater dependence on his suppliers in this respect, and less to contact with suppliers and flexibility of supply.

Allowing for differences in sample size, large and small retailers' assessment of the style, quality and performance of British as compared to

Table 4.2. *Analysis of replies to questionnaire by small firms retailing clothing and related products[a]*

| | Importance of purchasing factors | | Compared with foreign supplies British goods are: | | | | |
	No. of replies	% score	No. of replies	Better	About the same	Worse	Weighted balance
Price	73	68	71	7	32	32	−60
Style	75	91	71	11	34	26	−47
Quality	75	88	71	14	28½	28½	−46½
Performance	73	77	67	6	53	8	−4
Novelty	66	30	59	2	35	22	−24
Delivery	75	79	70	8	35	27	−48
Promotion	74	36	69	29	27	13	+15
Contact	74	49	70	32	30	8	+35
Knowledge	75	63	71	25	36	10	+22
Flexibility	75	55	71	23	36	12	+9

[a] All respondents sold clothing; roughly half sold other goods as well, chiefly household textiles, toys and leisure goods, or were mixed retailers.

foreign goods was similar, although small retailers were more critical of the quality of British goods and of their performance. The small retailers also found that British prices tended to be higher than foreign prices, but whereas this was judged to be the case by two out of every three large retailers only two out of five small firms judged British goods more expensive. Clearly, however, the small retailers were less satisfied with the service provided by British manufacturers. On delivery, those who found British manufacturers worse than suppliers of foreign goods outnumbered those who found them better; and a higher proportion of small respondents found British manufacturers worse on promotion, contact, knowledge of the market and flexibility of supply, even though in total British suppliers were thought as good as or better than their competitors. This dissatisfaction, which was common to all sub-groups among small retailers, was implicitly reinforced in their comments on the importance of packaging, the supply of promotional material, pre-season advertising and after-sales service. Several interviewees made similar points, confirming that British manufacturers do not treat their small customers as carefully as they do their large.

The firm that provided a detailed and instructive answer had five departments selling: fashions; linens, soft furnishings and dress fabrics; underwear, swimwear and leisurewear; children's wear; and china, glass and gifts. Averaging the five scores for purchasing factors gave a ranking close to that of shops selling a similar range of goods, with emphasis on quality, style and delivery. The only exceptional feature was an oddly low score for performance. The rankings were never identical between different departments, but the differences referred principally to service factors other than delivery rather than to price and product characteristics. The assessments of British as compared with foreign products and manufacturers was still more varied but on the whole good. They were rated as good or better on all counts except price by the fashion department, on all except delivery by linens, on all except flexibility of supply and novelty in underwear, and on all except price and again novelty in children's wear. The china, glass and gifts department, however, took a jaundiced view of things British: worse on style, novelty (very important here), delivery, promotion and flexibility of supply and about the same on everything else. This result provides an illustration of the diversity of replies given when product lines are separately distinguished and also perhaps, though this may be an unjust conclusion, of prejudice on the part of some buyers. In this instance, as for a number of small and indeed large retailers, British was worse; for some, though fewer, British was better for no apparent reason.

ELECTRONIC AND ELECTRICAL GOODS

The second large group of retailers replying to the questionnaires was small retailers of electronic consumer goods and domestic electric appliances. Out of a total of 109 respondents, 50 were selling electronic consumer goods, eleven domestic appliances and the rest both. 22 respondents were small multiples with two to nine outlets; the remainder were single-outlet retailers.

Their replies are summarised in table 4.3. Here performance and quality are the first considerations, style and appearance falls to third place, price ranks fourth, closely followed by delivery. The ranking is similar for all sub-groups except, rather oddly, in relation to price. For retailers of electronic consumer goods it ranked fifth, with 70 per cent, as also for retailers of domestic electric appliances. Firms selling both ranked price a close third to performance and quality which may be a reflection of the less specialised nature of their business. 28 out of the 47 respondents in this group said that price was very important and the remainder that it was important. Among the 50 retailers of electronic consumer goods only, sixteen indicated that it was very important and eleven that it was of some importance. On all the remaining purchasing factors the ranking was very similar, though the small number of retailers dealing in domestic electric appliances alone was more concerned than the rest with novelty and technological innovation, flexibility of supply and contact with suppliers. As compared with small clothing retailers, retailers of electrical and electronic goods were notably more concerned about supplier promotion, contact with suppliers and novelty.

Table 4.3. *Analysis of replies to questionnaire by small firms retailing electronic consumer goods and domestic electric appliances*

| | Importance of purchasing factors | | Compared with foreign supplies British goods are: | | | | |
	No. of replies	% score	No. of replies	Better	About the same	Worse	Weighted balance
Price	108	77	101	23	61	17	+10
Style	107	80	102	6	51½	44½	−93
Quality	108	88	99	6	52½	40½	−90½
Performance	109	89	102	7	61	34	−70
Novelty	106	48	99	6	47	46	−69
Delivery	108	75	99	19	55	25	−19
Promotion	109	69	101	23	56½	21½	− 6½
Contact	109	64	101	21	62	18	+ 9
Knowledge	108	69	102	19	66	17	− 4
Flexibility	109	62	101	20	66	15	− 6

Retailers of electrical and electronic goods took a decidedly poorer view of British goods and producers than did clothing retailers. British prices were thought to be lower by rather more respondents than thought them higher. This was almost entirely due to replies from retailers of domestic electric appliances; otherwise better and worse balanced out and a majority of retailers found them about the same. Those considering the design characteristics of British products worse always outnumbered those thinking them better, and sometimes came close to equalling the number of those who thought British design features were 'about the same' as those of their competitors. British manufacturers came out relatively better on service to retailers but hardly well, particularly on delivery. Specialist electronic retailers were particularly critical of service by British manufacturers.

Retailers in this market do, of course, demand more and more active support from their suppliers, as was very plain from the comments on other factors influencing purchases. Spares and after-sales service were frequently mentioned. (One retailer made the interesting observation that manufacturers who were farming out the supply of spares to special-ist companies were able to supply them more rapidly.) Almost as many retailers complained that margins were inadequate, particularly on Brit-ish goods. Such complaints were often coupled with the need for 'exclus-ivity': the small retailer cannot compete with the multiples selling the same brands. A few respondents enlarged on the design defects of British products: 'in brown goods (electronics) the United Kingdom range is limited and perceived value for money inferior'; 'the British are making a budget TV – the customer will only buy cheap once'; 'foreign products command a better price by good design'.

It proved impossible to secure replies from a sufficient number of large retailers in this sector, especially retailers of electronic consumer goods, to permit numerical analysis without breach of confidence; but those replies that were obtained, the majority relating to electrical rather than electronic goods, tended to suggest that their ranking of purchasing factors was very close to that of small retailers, save that they gave greater importance to delivery, to (rather oddly) promotion and to novelty and technological innovation. They took a more favourable view of goods produced in the United Kingdom, finding quality and performance as good as or better than those of imported goods and were less critical of style, though still finding the style and appearance of imported goods superior to the domestic product. They were also more inclined to find British prices lower and usually found delivery as good or better. Like the large clothing retailers, large electrical retailers received better service from their British suppliers (nearly always rated better than or about the same as their competitors) than did small retailers.

OTHER HOUSEHOLD GOODS

In table 4.4, replies from 24 small retailers of a variety of household goods are summarised. The products sold include carpets, furniture, household textiles, china and glassware, domestic metalware, hardware and ironmongery and do-it-yourself goods. Most of the retailers concerned sold several types of products, including a few falling outside the broad classification of household goods. This both made it difficult for respondents to give meaningful replies, and to analyse them. One respondent helpfully gave separate replies on price and on style and

Table 4.4. *Analysis of replies to questionnaire by small firms retailing household goods*

| | Importance of purchasing factors | | Compared with foreign supplies British goods are: | | | | |
	No. of replies	% score	No. of replies	Better	About the same	Worse	Weighted balance
Price	24	76	22	2	13	7	−13
Style	24	89	20	6	9	5	+ 2
Quality	23	93	21	6	8	7	− 5
Performance	24	85	20	2	16	2	− 1
Novelty	23	36	19	1	11½	6½	− 4½
Delivery	24	79	21	4	8	9	−13
Promotion	24	51	20	10	7	3	+ 5
Contact	24	50	21	10	9	2	+ 7
Knowledge	23	54	21	4	15	2	+ 5
Flexibility	24	57	21	5	12	4	0

Table 4.5. *Analysis of replies to questionnaire by large firms retailing household goods*

	Importance of purchasing factors		Compared with foreign supplies British goods are:				
	No. of replies	% score	No. of replies	Better	About the same	Worse	Weighted balance
Price	39	81	39	6	13	20	$-37\frac{1}{2}$
Style	39	92	39	16	$21\frac{1}{2}$	$1\frac{1}{2}$	$+39\frac{1}{2}$
Quality	39	86	39	$13\frac{5}{6}$	$24\frac{5}{6}$	$\frac{1}{3}$	$+37\frac{1}{2}$
Performance	39	83	39	8	31	0	$+21$
Novelty	39	40	36	3	23	10	-8
Delivery	39	91	39	10	21	8	$+12$
Promotion	39	35	37	26	9	2	$+30$
Contact	39	72	39	24	14	1	$+47$
Knowledge	39	68	39	27	9	3	$+41$
Flexibility	39	72	39	17	17	5	$+21$

appearance for different product lines. Both, for example, were considered very important for domestic electric appliances, important for hardware, of some importance for domestic metalware and did not matter for ironmongery. Other products varied but the average was: important for price, some importance for style and appearance, which is clearly not a meaningful result.

For the group as a whole, quality scored highest as a purchasing factor, closely followed by style and appearance and by performance. Looking only at those retailers who sold china and glassware, whether or not they sold other goods as well, style and appearance were more important; for those retailers dealing in furniture and carpets quality and performance led, while for retailers concentrating on DIY goods, hardware and domestic metalware quality was paramount. United Kingdom products tended to be judged worse on style by retailers of china, worse on quality by retailers of furniture and carpets but better on both quality and style by firms concentrating on hardware and related products. It was this latter group too that was largely responsible for the poor showing of British goods on price, though not all retailers of china were happy with British prices; among retailers selling furniture and carpets, United Kingdom prices were almost without exception judged to be about the same as the prices of imported goods. On other points, particularly on the familiar inferiority of British firms' performance on delivery, the answers were similar, regardless of the different types of retailing and goods involved.

Table 4.5 analyses 39 replies from large retailers dealing in furniture and carpets, household textiles, china and earthenware, domestic metalware, and wallcoverings. The questionnaires related to specific products or product groups; the replies are therefore more nearly exact. As might be expected, import dependence tended to be less for furniture, china and wallcoverings than for other goods in the group, and on the high side for household textiles and domestic metalware. All sectors of the market in terms of age and class were covered. Large retailers of household goods appear to give slightly greater weight to style and appearance and to price, slightly less to quality and performance than their small competitors; but the real difference between the two groups lies in the importance attached to services provided by manufacturers. The large retailers give greater weight not only to speed and reliability of delivery, but also to flexibility of supply, to close contact with suppliers and to the latters' knowledge of the market. The most probable explanation is that whereas for small retailers a good deal of this filters through via the wholesalers with whom they deal, the large retailers dealing entirely with manufacturers and importers expect them to do more of the work.

Large retailers are in general much better satisfied with the design features of British goods, except as always novelty, and with the service provided by British manufacturers than are small household goods retailers and indeed than any other group surveyed. British prices are the great stumbling block, and this is true of all the products covered save wallcoverings. To sum up: design is the first thing that most retailers look at when purchasing goods. The emphasis on style and appearance, quality and product performance varies as between retailers according to the goods concerned and according to the firm's market and policy but one or more of these factors is rated more highly than price by every one of the groups of retailers that replied to the questionnaire. Price is important, for some retailers very important, but it is no more than one element in a complex process of choice. The other critical factor for the majority of retailers is speedy and reliable delivery. The remaining service factors (supplier promotion, close and frequent contact with suppliers, their knowledge of the market and flexibility of supply) matter less, though they are still important, particularly to the smaller retailer and to less specialised firms. Novelty and technological innovation are important only to comparatively few purchasers, who are generally operating in specialised market sectors.

British importers show a remarkably similar pattern of preference. Thanks to the assistance of the British Importers Confederation, it was possible to canvass importers' views on purchasing factors. They were asked to complete question 1 of the retailers' questionnaire and 27 did so. Half were importers of clothing and footwear, the remainder imported a wide range of goods. Nearly all were importing from Western Europe and/or the Far East and a few from other areas also; and most of them sold to retailers of many kinds as well as to manufacturers and wholesalers, save a few subsidiaries that were importing on behalf of their related parents. The score was (in per cent of the possible total):

Price	82	Delivery	82
Style and appearance	94	Supplier promotion	7
Quality	95	Contact with supplier	74
Product performance	89	Supplier's knowledge of	
Novelty/technological		market	43
innovation	46	Flexibility of supply	46

Once again, style, quality and product performance are the most important factors in making decisions to purchase. It is disquieting, therefore, that judging by figures derived by summing all the replies analysed in tables 4.1 to 4.5, one in three retailers find British products worse than imported goods in style and appearance and in quality, and one in five find them worse on performance. Roughly half of all retailers (more in the case of product performance) consider British goods about the same, leaving 15 per cent or less thinking them better than the competition. On price and delivery the proportions are similar. Rather more than one in three retailers judged British prices higher; just under one in three found British performance on delivery worse; half found them about the same; and a minority found them cheaper and better.

REASONS FOR IMPORTING: THE LARGE RETAILERS

Among the large retailers, the share of imports in purchases is loosely related to the view taken of British goods and manufacturers. Replies from 26 firms with exceptionally low import dependence and 35 with exceptionally high dependence are summarised in table 4.6. (Not all respondents covered all points.) The low importers almost always find British goods and producers as good as, or better than, their competitors; although on novelty those finding them worse slightly outnumber those finding them better, while there is no factor on which at least one of the group does not rate British worse. In the right-hand half of the table, the high importers find British prices, style, quality, novelty and delivery worse more often than better, although on the remaining factors the reverse is true.

However, practice does not necessarily follow judgement. Because of the greater ease and convenience of purchasing domestic rather than imported products, there has to be a wide difference in the price and

Table 4.6. *Assessment of British goods by large retailers with exceptionally low or high import dependence*

	26 Low[a] importers: British goods are:			35 High[b] importers: British goods are:		
	Better	About the same	Worse	Better	About the same	Worse
Price	$9\frac{1}{2}$	$10\frac{1}{2}$	6	4	$10\frac{1}{2}$	$20\frac{1}{2}$
Style	13	10	2	$1\frac{1}{3}$	$18\frac{1}{3}$	$16\frac{1}{3}$
Quality	6	16	4	$7\frac{1}{3}$	$17\frac{5}{6}$	$10\frac{5}{6}$
Performance	4	20	2	7	26	2
Novelty/ technology	4	11	8	$2\frac{1}{2}$	$16\frac{1}{2}$	15
Delivery	$11\frac{1}{2}$	$11\frac{1}{2}$	3	$6\frac{1}{2}$	17	$12\frac{1}{2}$
Promotion	13	8	3	14	12	4
Contact	16	9	1	14	21	1
Knowledge	17	6	2	14	17	4
Flexibility	17	7	2	11	12	11

[a] Less than 10 per cent of supplies.
[b] Over 40 per cent of supplies.

design of British and imported goods before retailers resort to imported supplies for other reasons than to widen the range of products on offer and supply specialist products not made in Britain such as French perfumes. (One retailer interviewed suggested that domestic producers had a built-in price advantage of as much as 20 per cent over competing imports because of the extra cost and difficulty involved in importing.) In the questionnaires sent to large retailers and in interviews, retailers were asked their reasons for purchasing imported rather than British goods. Is it because imported goods are cheaper; because they are superior in design and quality; because foreign suppliers and importers are easier to deal with than British producers; or because comparable goods are not made in the United Kingdom? As before, they were also asked to mention any other reasons.

Replies were received from 109 retailers and retail buyers, of whom 48 were dealing in clothing and footwear, 38 in household goods, and most of the remainder in electrical products. Replies from five retailers of other goods not covered in previous sections of this chapter were also included in the total. Many respondents gave more than one reason for importing so that altogether there were 173 replies under the four headings specified above plus a few others. One respondent mentioned the superior reliability of foreign suppliers; the remainder referred to the non-availability of certain products in the United Kingdom because of the lack of specific skills and materials in the production of clothing and footwear, to exclusivity and better foreign ranges.

In 72 cases, the lack of comparable British-made products was mentioned, in 60 price, in 35 inferior British design and quality which was cited particularly often by retailers of clothing, and in half a dozen the greater difficulty of dealing with British suppliers. This last reason was mentioned mainly in relation to household textiles; most retailers ignored it. There is, of course, a subjective element in these replies. It is perhaps particularly difficult to distinguish between 'design' and 'availability'. One retailer may mark design where another would judge that the required design was 'not available'. Likewise one retailer might mark price if British products were not available at that price, whereas another might indicate 'not available'. Further investigation suggested, however, that respondents clearly distinguished between factors.

The analysis was repeated for retailers with exceptionally low or high shares of imports in purchases, and for those catering to the upper and lower ends of the income range, ignoring other respondents. The pattern of replies from low (less than 10 per cent) and high (over 40 per cent) importers showed high importers being much more likely to purchase overseas because of design than were low importers, but this may have been because retailers of clothing were rather over-represented in the former group and of household goods in the latter; the low importers gave greater weight to non-availability and to price. The comparison between retailers to higher and lower income groups was more revealing. Out of 31 retailers who identified themselves as catering wholly or to a significant degree to social classes A and B, non-availability was mentioned 25 times as the reason for importing (principally by retailers of clothing and footwear), inferior British design seventeen times and price twelve times. Among the 31 retailers catering wholly or in part to social classes D and E, price was mentioned 23 times, non-availability sixteen, but design only four times. In other words, three quarters of the replies from retailers to lower income groups but less than two fifths of those from retailers to upper income groups gave price as a reason for importing. Higher up the market both design and non-availability are more frequently the motive for foreign purchases.

The sample is too small to warrant any hard and fast conclusions; but it does suggest that rising incomes offer greater opportunities to British manufacturers of consumer goods, provided that design can be improved. In many lines they cannot compete on price at the lower end of the market. Apparently there are already a good many manufacturers competing successfully on price at the upper end.

5

CLOTHING AND KNITWEAR

Clothing and knitwear are classified as separate industries, the latter being regarded as part of the textile industry, but they meet the same demand and the larger United Kingdom producers straddle both industries, as well as other textile sectors. It is convenient, therefore, to take a broad view of both together, before examining certain specific products. United Kingdom manufacturers' deliveries of clothing were estimated at £3,513 million in 1984, of hosiery and knitwear at £1,340 million. Retail sales including imports, valued at retail prices including VAT, were estimated at £10,294 million, of which £3,942 million or 34 per cent was men's and boys' wear, £5,754 million or 56 per cent women's and girls' wear, and £781 million or 8 per cent children's wear. The balance was made up of clothing materials and haberdashery.

Total clothing expenditure has broadly followed the trend of all consumer spending in real terms, although as noted in Chapter 2 it has been less buoyant than spending on electrical and electronic goods, and more resilient than expenditure on other household goods. Within the total, however, demand for menswear and womenswear developed very differently, as may be seen from table 5.1. In terms of the volume of production, non-knit clothing achieved a remarkably good performance in the late 1970s, but output collapsed in the recession and only by 1985 had it recovered to nearly the 1979 level. The knitwear industry has fared much worse. The change in coverage of the production index at 1978 is greater than for clothing, so precisely how output has developed is uncertain; but it appears that production may have peaked around 1977. Thereafter it fell year by year to 1982 and, though it has since recovered, output is well below the levels achieved in the 1970s. Even so, its performance is little worse than the average for all consumer goods industries, while that of the clothing industry is among the best outside the electronic/electrical sector.

Both before and after 1979, import penetration rose more in knitwear than in non-knit clothing. Until 1979, however, any loss of sales due to the rise in clothing imports was almost wholly offset by higher exports and an improvement in the balance of trade relative to supplies. In knitwear the balance deteriorated, which accounts for the slower growth

Table 5.1. *Indicators of demand and output in the clothing and knitwear industries*

1980 = 100

	Consumers' expenditure at 1980 prices			Output	
	Menswear	Womes's & infants' wear[a]	Total	Clothing	Knitwear
1974	105.0	73.5	84.0	100.7	109.6
1975	103.3	75.5	84.8	101.7	106.5
1976	100.6	76.8	85.0	98.0	112.5
1977	99.2	79.5	86.1	104.6 —[b]	112.9 —[b]
1978	103.6	88.6	93.6	108.3	110.6
1979	106.4	97.4	100.4	110.7	108.3
1980	100	100	100	100	100
1981	98.2	100.7	100.0	92.4	96.4
1982	103.5	102.3	102.7	93.8	94.6
1983	112.6	109.0	110.2	96.9	95.2
1984	123.7	113.7	117.1	103.7	96.9
1985	131.3	123.9	126.4	110.3	99.4

Source: See Appendix I.
[a] Including clothing materials and haberdashery.
[b] Bars denote break in series.

Table 5.2. *Import penetration and the balance of trade: clothing and knitwear*

	Imports as per cent of apparent consumption		Trade balance as per cent of supplies	
	Clothing	Knitwear	Clothing	Knitwear
1974	20[a]	14	−10[a]	−1
1975	22[a]	18	−11[a]	−3
1976	22[a]	22	−10[a]	−3
1977	21[a] —[b]	22 —[b]	−5[a] —[b]	−1 —[b]
1978	25	25	−7	−4
1979	28	28	−9	−6
1980	29 —[b]	30	−9	−5
1981	31	34	−12	−8
1982	31	33	−13	−8
1983	31	34	−13	−9
1984	33	38	−16	−12
1985	34	36	−14	−8

Source: See Appendix 1.
[a] Estimated.
[b] Bars denote break in series.

of output between 1974 and 1979. From 1979 to 1984, the clothing
industry lost out on both sides of the trade account. Had the import
penetration ratio remained constant, deliveries at current prices would
have been 6 per cent higher in 1984 than they actually were, and if
the ratio of exports to output had been held at the 1979 level, a further
2.4 per cent would have been added to deliveries.

Rather surprisingly, the total loss of knitwear deliveries calculated
in the same way was almost exactly the same proportion of 1984 deliveries, with a bigger loss on imports partly recouped by a rise in exports
relative to output. Since apparent consumption measured in current
prices was rising at very similar rates in both industries, the explanation
of differences in the rate of output growth probably lies in the behaviour
of prices. Comparing two industries, if domestic prices rise faster, or
fall less, in relation to import prices in one, then an identical change
in import penetration measured in current prices will have a more serious
effect on the volume of output in the industry with the greater relative
price increase. In the absence of any adequate data on producer prices
of all clothing and knitwear, this interpretation cannot be confirmed;
but it is reasonable to conclude that knitwear output has suffered more
from import penetration than all non-knit clothing, because its price
performance has been worse relative to its overseas competitors. This
would not be true in comparison with some sectors of the non-knit clothing industry. Differences in sectoral import penetration ratios provide
a rough guide to competitiveness. In 1984 they were close to 45 per
cent for tailored outerwear, both men's and women's, a little under 40
per cent for weatherproof outerwear and shirts, 31 per cent for work
clothing and jeans, and 23 per cent for women's lightweight outerwear,
lingerie and children's wear.

The pattern of imports is complex. Both industries are so to speak
fighting on two fronts, under severe competitive pressure from the new
industrial countries in the Far East and from European suppliers; while
established suppliers in the Far East are themselves coming under pressure from new producers developing their clothing sales to the United
Kingdom, as British importers hunt for new sources of supply to beat
the limits imposed by the MFA.[1] In 1984, the EC including Greece
supplied 32.5 per cent of all imports of clothing and knitwear by value,
EFTA 10.4 per cent, of which 5.8 per cent came from Portugal. 36.7
per cent came from the four main Asian suppliers – Hong Kong, South
Korea, Taiwan and India. Hong Kong alone provided 23.2 per cent
of imports. Among the newcomers Turkey has perhaps been the most
successful with 2.2 per cent of imports in 1984. Like other newcomers,
its sales are concentrated in one or two lines. It supplied for example
almost a quarter of all cotton knitted shirts and underwear (mostly in

Table 5.3. *United Kingdom clothing and knitwear imports: selected items, 1984*

	Of cotton and man-made fibres			Of wool and other fibres	
	Value £mn	EC share %	Hong Kong share %	Value £mn	EC share %
Non-knit clothing					
Menswear: coats & jackets	33.8	25	...	22.8	52
trousers	192.2	22	43	10.1	64
suits	33.1	36	...	43.3	66
other outerwear	97.2	18	37	4.2	93
shirts & underwear	145.2	13	46	2.7	63
Total men's & boys' wear	501.5	20	...	83.1	63
Womenswear: dresses	62.9	53	17	14.6	80
coats, jackets, skirts	83.1	45	...	35.6	75
blouses	70.6	26	31	5.4	63
other outerwear	174.5	32	35	27.0	79
underwear	17.6	26	...	1.1	64
Total women's, girls' & children's wear	408.7	37	...	83.7	77
Knitted clothing					
Jerseys, pullovers, etc.	204.8	32	18	81.7	40
Dresses, skirts, suits, etc.	34.0	41	16	5.7	61
Men's shirts	25.1	10	45	...	...
Other	248.2	23	...	10.5	57
Total knitted clothing	512.1	27	...	97.9	43

Source: See Appendix 1.

fact T-shirts). The migrant workers sent back from Germany are developing production rapidly with the help of German capital and exceptionally favourable treatment under the MFA.

Table 5.3 illustrates the pattern of trade of the main sectors of the clothing industry. Specialised items such as leather and rubber clothing, proofed garments, gloves and so forth, many of which tend to come from rather different groups of suppliers, are omitted. Broadly speaking, the origin of imports varies according to the material used, the degree of standardisation and the complexity of the manufacturing process. Thus the Community and other industrial countries have a higher share in wool clothing than in clothing of cotton and man-made fibres, in non-knit than in knitted clothing, in womenswear than in menswear. Apart, however, from shirts and a few other items, they have a substantial share of imports in all clothing sectors, supplying high-quality and high-fashion goods. The Asian NICs have diversified and traded up under the pressure of competition from the developing countries; they too now supply some high-fashion goods as well as a huge volume of standard products. It is largely left to the newcomers to supply the bottom of the market.

Since the currencies of most of the major Far Eastern producers are linked more or less closely to the dollar, and the United States is their main market, the pound's rate of exchange against the dollar as well as against West European currencies has an important influence on competition. When the dollar was riding high and demand in the United States was strong, Far Eastern suppliers concentrated on the American market. As demand there slackens and the dollar falls, it is feared that competition from the Far East in Europe, and especially in Britain, will become more intense. The possible scale of this effect is indicated by the fact that as the dollar rose, the share of the three major Far Eastern producers – Hong Kong, South Korea and Taiwan – in United Kingdom imports fell from 35 per cent in 1981 to 29 per cent in 1985, though this may also reflect loss of confidence in Hong Kong at the time of the Anglo-Chinese negotiations. In 1985, indeed, Far Eastern sales to the United Kingdom fell in absolute terms, accounting for most of the decline in the value of imports in that year. Imports from Western Europe, by contrast, continued to rise. Germany in particular has made rapid headway as a supplier of quality clothing.

MANUFACTURERS AND RETAILERS

Both clothing and knitwear firms suffered severely in the recession. The Census of Production records a drop of 17 per cent in the number of clothing enterprises from 6,947 to 5,761 between 1979 and 1983, and of 11 per cent in knitwear firms from 944 to 840. The fall was exceptionally severe in men's and women's tailored outerwear, where employment fell by more than 40 per cent as against 29 per cent for all non-knit clothing and 21 per cent in knitwear. Capital spending was cut back, but has picked up again, particularly in clothing. Larger firms are going all out to catch up with Continental producers and increase productivity through the introduction of more capital-intensive methods of production, adding to the very big rise already achieved by cutting out dead wood in the recession.

Some very large firms are involved in production, and they are becoming still larger, thanks to recent mergers. In 1985 Vanton Viyella merged with Nottingham Manufacturing and a year later the group merged with Coats Patons to become Coats Viyella, one of the largest textile companies in the world, let alone Europe, with a combined turnover of £1.7 billion. Turnover in clothing is of course much smaller, of the order of £450 million to £500 million, including non-British turnover. Other giants operating in the industry are Courtaulds, with clothing turnover in excess of £400 million, and Tootals with rather smaller clothing sales. William Baird is probably the fourth largest clothing manufacturer, with turnover comfortably exceeding £200 million. There are several large but more specialised companies with turnover now coming close to £100 million, such as the Lee Cooper group, Corah and Gent. Many of these firms have characteristics in common besides, for consumer goods producers, large size. They have turned their backs on the excessive centralisation of the 1970s which got them into serious trouble, and their subsidiaries are allowed greater freedom in order to maintain contact with the market; all are becoming deliberately market-oriented and some at least are increasing their design capability. They generally produce both their own named brands and supply retailers' brands under contract, in addition to exporting. Branded goods are sold principally through department stores and independents, and in the case of Coats through its own Jaeger and Country Casual outlets; a high proportion of contract work is for Marks and Spencer, the country's largest retailer of clothing, which boasts that 90 per cent of its merchandise is British made. Besides the big producers there are several medium-sized companies with a strong brand identity and often their own retail outlets – shops or concessions – such as, for example, Aquascutum. In general, however, the share of manufacturers' brands in the market is low, a marked contrast to the situation in Germany where manufacturers' brands dominate the market.

Beyond the large and medium-sized producers, there is a crowd of small and very small firms. According to the 1984 Census of Production, 8,463 enterprises employing fewer than 100 persons contributed close on two fifths of output in the clothing industry. At the other end of the scale, 64 establishments employing 500 or more contributed very slightly more to output but turnover in most cases was less than £20 million. The Stock Exchange listed only sixteen companies in 1984 with turnover exceeding £20 million, apart from the big textile groups. Comparable data for knitwear include firms specialising in warp knitted goods rather than supplying clothing: 62 out of a total of 902 classified to the knitting industry as a whole. Of this total, 32 firms employing more than 500 accounted for 56 per cent of output, 1,338 with fewer than 100 employees supplied 21 per cent. As might be expected, concentration in knitting is much higher than in clothing, although not high in any absolute sense. The five largest knitting enterprises produced 31 per cent of output in 1983, the five largest clothing enterprises a mere 13 per cent, making it one of the least concentrated consumer goods industries that there is.

The large firm is much more important in retailing. The share of multiple retailers has been rising steadily over the past decade, reaching 59 per cent for all clothing in 1984 against (a possibly overstated) 53 per cent in 1976. Most of the gain has accrued to multiples with a hundred or more outlets, who carried on 39 per cent of the clothing trade in 1984. Small retailers, more especially the small multiples with between two and nine outlets, have lost particularly heavily in womenswear, where their share of the market fell by 7 per cent; in menswear it fell only 3 per cent. By 1984, the single-outlet retailers had 26 per cent of all retail sales, and rather more of womenswear, while the small multiples had 15 per cent with a rather higher share in menswear. Concentration in retailing is slightly above average and certainly higher than in production, with the top five sellers of menswear accounting for 36 per cent of 1984 sales and the top five sellers of womenswear for 31 per cent.

The Retail Enquiry makes an artificial distinction between retailing of men's and of women's and children's clothes which in practice does not exist: almost all the very big retailers of clothing sell both. Adding together the average turnover of the five largest retailers in each category in 1984 gives a figure of £667 million, including VAT, for the biggest clothing retailers, or say £580–90 million excluding VAT. Marks and Spencer's United Kingdom clothing sales in the financial year equivalent to calendar year 1984 are estimated to have been of the order of £1.4 billion, excluding VAT; Burton, which was probably among the top five then, had a clothing turnover estimated at £360 million excluding VAT. (It is very much larger now, over £1 billion in 1986, making Burton the second largest retailer of clothing after Marks and Spencer.) This would leave average turnover of £400 million or so for the remaining members of the big five, and the next five largest retailers would have had average turnover in excess of £200 million. Apart from Marks and Spencer and Burton, clothing turnover of the major retailers cannot be estimated but it is likely that in 1984 they included such firms as GUS, Sears and Littlewoods, BHS as it then was, C. & A., House of Fraser, perhaps John Lewis and the then independent Debenhams. All these firms had very large turnover in clothing, and most of them had total turnover in excess of £500 million, some approaching or exceeding £1 billion. In short, the major customers of clothing manufacturers were very large and powerful retailers, with enormous buying power.

Indeed, it appears that on average the purchases of the largest retailers of clothing in 1984 were more than twice as large as the sales of the largest manufacturers in the clothing and knitwear industries. The ratio of one to the other can be very roughly calculated by reference to the average turnover of the five largest manufacturers and the five largest retailers. The former can be derived directly from concentration data in the Census of Production, which gives aggregate sales and work done by the five largest enterprises in each 3-digit industry. To derive a figure for retail purchases requires some manipulation of the concentration data in the Retail Enquiry, which covers sales including VAT and gross margin, by commodity, whereas purchases are equivalent to sales net of VAT, margin and changes in stocks which are available only by kinds of business. In order to estimate average purchases by the top five retailers, the incidence of VAT and margin for the kind of retail business specialising in the goods concerned has been calculated and applied to the commodity sales figures to give a rough estimate of purchases. Stock changes have been ignored, as has the fact that among specialist retailers, gross margins tend to increase with size of business. The ratio is thus a very crude indicator but it has the great advantage that it is possible to compare the position across a number of industries as is done in subsequent chapters.

Summing estimated purchases of menswear and womenswear, the ratio of average purchases by the five largest retailers to sales by the five largest manufacturers of clothing is just under, and of knitwear just over, 4:1. Taking purchases of menswear and womenswear separately, the ratios are under 1.5 and over 2.5 respectively. In practice, of course, no retailer will absorb the entire output of one supplier (though they may sometimes come close to it) because purchases will cover a wide range of clothing sold by different manufacturers. But the fact remains that potentially the big retailers have the power to make or break manufacturers dependent on them for the greater part of their sales, a power that has been enhanced by the development of own brand retailing and by increasing centralisation of purchasing. Marks and Spencer, though a demanding customer with regard to price and quality, is known to be scrupulous in its treatment of suppliers; it is widely suggested that at least some other large firms are not. Developments in 1985 and 1986 have increased the size and strength of the largest clothing and knitwear manufacturers, but a serious imbalance between retailer and most manufacturers remains.

The mismatch in size is seen as a problem by both manufacturers and retailers, and certainly contributed to the bad relations between the two that developed in the late 1970s. When the going was good, retailers squeezed manufacturers; when manufacturers were sought after they retaliated. Poor training and qualifications among retail buyers exacerbated the situation. Latterly there has been a change for the better, for a number of reasons. Hard times in the recession led to an all-round improvement in manufacturers' performance, particularly among the larger firms. Communications between manufacturers and retailers have also improved. For this it appears that the Joint Textile Committee and the Clothing and Knitting EDCs can take a good deal of credit. They have sponsored a manufacturer–retailer panel on which both sides are represented. Coverage is necessarily incomplete because of the fragmented nature of the industry and of part of retailing; but at least the panel, whose remit is to look at future opportunities in terms of import substitution, has successfully promoted the discussion of problems by the larger retailers and any manufacturers prepared to meet them. The EDC's other initiative, the 'Better made in Britain' campaign, designed to show manufacturers that they can replace goods currently imported by retailers with their own products, may also have been of some use.

It is probable, however, that what has been most important in this context is the development of a new style of retailing combined with changes in fashion and buying habits. The changes include the introduction of what has been described as 'lifestyle retailing' – the sale of carefully co-ordinated garments in coherent colours and styles; a shift from the traditional two fashion seasons to four or more, or to the phased introduction of a range; lower stockholding and hence shorter lead times and more frequent purchasing; and in consequence closer relations between manufacturer and retailer. The prime example of this approach is Next, which employs designers in its buying department who work closely with manufacturers' own designers. Its success has prompted other retailers to follow its example. The introduction of EPOS (electronic point of sale systems) permits more precise analysis of sales and demand and is expected to lead to still closer relations, with manufacturers linked into retail computer networks. It is expected that all this will strengthen the hand of nearby producers over Far Eastern suppliers, of Continental and Mediterranean producers as well as domestic manufacturers. But though manufacturer–retailer relations are becoming closer, the market still remains and will continue to be retail-led.

Changes among the large producers and retailers still leave the small manufacturer out in the cold. The typical small firm is deficient both in adequately trained personnel and financial resources, with neither the time nor the money to invest in design and marketing. Their problems have been aggravated by the decline of traditional wholesaling. Large retailers do most of their own wholesaling or expect manufacturers to do it for them, although enquiries among retailers proved that wholesalers are still used to some extent, even by very big firms. The small, independent retailer still depends fairly heavily on wholesalers, but among the questionnaire replies from small retailers dealing exclusively in clothing, less than half reported that they dealt with wholesalers whereas all dealt directly with United Kingdom manufacturers and almost all with the representatives of foreign manufacturers.

Pure wholesaling, involving stockholding and selling, is thought now to account for only 10 to 15 per cent of trade in clothing. The contraction of wholesaling is attributed to pressure on margins, bad management and inefficiency on the part of the wholesaler; and to the purchase and, when heavy losses were made, subsequent closure of wholesalers by

Courtaulds during the 1970s, when it was attempting to create a highly integrated business. It was also suggested that much traditional wholesaling was replaced by cash-and-carry but no evidence was found to support this view. Small retailers resorted to cash-and-carry wholesalers even less than to wholesalers proper. Thus the manufacturer is constrained to deal primarily with the retailer. It could be helpful to the small manufacturer were wholesaling to revive, but it is hard to imagine how that could be achieved. An apparently obvious solution to the problem of selling – a common sales organisation for small producers – has been tried and so far failed, because of underfunding and because of suspicion and competition between members. This latter seems to be endemic in the more traditional small firm sector; the same situation was encountered in other industries. New small firms, many of them highly successful, suffer less from this particular problem because they are inclined to be market-oriented rather than production-oriented from the start.

REASONS FOR IMPORTING

It is generally thought that the great bulk of imports is handled directly by the larger retailers who import on their own account. They certainly import directly, but they also obtain imported goods through other channels. Of the large clothing retailers who were consulted about their business in general, almost all imported direct; the exceptions were involved in very specialised aspects of the clothing trade. About half the large retailers, however, obtained additional supplies from wholesalers and importers, and also reported that they purchased imported goods from manufacturers who were themselves importers. Imports are bought in by manufacturers to complete or supplement the range of goods offered for sale. A similar pattern was found among the retailers questioned about specific products, which are discussed below. Almost all imported directly and via manufacturers; some additionally had recourse to import merchants and wholesalers. Thus even among the big retailers, whether specialists or mixed businesses, there is no consistent pattern, while among the small retailers there is, as we have seen, greater reliance on wholesalers and also on importers. It is impossible to determine what proportion of imports passes through the different channels.

The reason for importing given by the larger retailers in general was most commonly that comparable goods were not available in the United Kingdom. Only half as many referred to price or design. As regards design, this was clearly a real reason rather than any confusion between 'design' and 'availability', since most of those who mentioned the former also specified the latter as a reason for importing. Because of the rather up-market character of the sample, the role of price in importing may have been understated. Certainly there is a huge volume of low-price imports mainly intended for the lower end of the market where, it is believed, import penetration is particularly high. A majority of large retailers found British prices higher than those of imports, as did two fifths of small clothing retailers and neither group was entirely happy with the style and quality of British goods; save on delivery they were for the most part satisfied with the service provided by British firms, as were those retailers consulted about specific products.

Manufacturers took an almost identical view of the reasons for import penetration, stressing price, style and delivery, and quality in that order. Points that were mentioned as being of particular importance for the small retailer were active selling by foreign firms, sales promotion and exclusivity, confirming what the small retailers themselves said. Another point specifically mentioned was difficulty experienced by British manufacturers in obtaining suitable fabrics. British cloth-producing capacity, already dented by import competition, was reduced in the recession, and British producers have concentrated more on non-clothing fabrics than have firms in the rest of Europe. It was also suggested that mass market retailing has accustomed the consumer to expect low prices but tolerate poor quality and design. The structure of demand in other West European countries is quite different; customers pay and expect more, so that there is a wider market for more expensive goods of better quality.

Manufacturers were asked why import penetration in the non-retail market should be lower than in the retail market, a query prompted by its relatively low level in that sector of the clothing industry producing work clothing and jeans, and by the evident conviction of the statisticians who prepared the 1979 Input–Output table that non-retail markets for consumer goods in general were less open to imports than retail markets for the same or similar products. The reasons are that workwear is made to very precise specifications, and closeness to the customer is required. Further, this sector of the industry, which is almost solely concerned with workwear, is extremely competitive. That the need to be close to the customer provides part of the defence against import competition in workwear is relevant to the industry as a whole, especially in the light of emerging developments in manufacturer–retailer relations already discussed.

The rest of this chapter is directed to an examination of import penetration in relation to three specific products: men's suits, women's blouses, and knitted jerseys and cardigans.

MEN'S SUITS

Precise data on import penetration in relation to men's and boys' woven suits are available only since 1980. In that year, imports accounted for

41 per cent by value of apparent consumption in the United Kingdom. The ratio rose sharply in 1981 and by 1982 was 52 per cent. It was held briefly, and then rose again in 1984 and 1985 to 57 per cent. The growth of import penetration by volume followed a similar course but at a higher level, rising from 53 per cent in 1980 to 70 per cent in 1985. The volume of imports has risen erratically, growing particularly sharply in 1981 and 1984.

Because of their higher price, wool suits account for more than half of total imports by value, but less than half by volume; the EC with Italy in the lead provided over 60 per cent of the value of imports in 1985. Suits of man-made fibres are the other major category of imports, greater in number but only some three quarters of the value of imports of wool suits. The Community's share of imports of suits of man-made fibres was not much over one third, whereas Yugoslavia alone provided more than a quarter. Romania is another important East European supplier and also exports wool suits to the United Kingdom. A number of smaller European countries, notably Portugal whose sales are increasing very rapidly, are also important suppliers and the balance comes from the Far East. East European and Far Eastern prices are extremely low by comparison with EC goods. The unit value of Romanian suits, for example, is less than half that of a suit made of the same fibre from the Community; and although this may be exceptional, reflecting dumping, it would be true to say that prices from the low-cost suppliers are at most two thirds of the price of a Community suit, and correspondingly low in relation to British prices.

The initial impetus to large-scale importing of suits may have been given by the shrinkage of the traditional made-to-measure market in the 1970s as retailers closed their associated factories in the face of mounting losses; but imports continued to rise because British prices moved out of line with those of foreign suppliers. According to the British Clothing Industry Association (BCIA), the average ex-factory price of a suit manufactured in the United Kingdom in 1977 was £25.37 and the average unit value of an imported suit was £20, giving a ratio of domestic to foreign price of 1.27. (These figures refer to all suits and take no account of differences in the cloth of which they are made.) By 1981 the ratio had risen to 1.69. British suits were then unable to compete on price with those from the Community, let alone with the products of low-cost producers. By 1985 the average ratio had improved but only to 1.62, still way above the 1977 ratio. In relation to Community products, the improvement was much greater, but the ratio had still not returned to where it had been. Unit values are tricky measures but they do make it plain that the gap between prices of low-cost and British suppliers is too wide to be filled, and they suggest that further improvements in price competitiveness are necessary to prevent further big increases in import penetration.

Retailers of men's suits gave almost equal weight to price, style, quality, performance and delivery in their purchases, with performance slightly in the lead and price a little behind the rest. Unusually for large retailers, they gave the same kind of weight to close contact with suppliers, the latter's knowledge of the market and flexibility of supply. Almost all the retailers consulted imported direct and several of them also made use of import merchants and wholesalers or purchased imported goods from manufacturers. The share of imports in purchases ranged between 10 and 40 per cent. Imports came chiefly from Western or Eastern Europe, with a little from the Far East, but there was no discernible tendency for retailers in particular market sectors to purchase in particular areas.

In almost every respect British products and producers were judged as good as or better than foreign products and producers, with the one serious exception of price. There was near unanimity that British prices were higher than foreign; only towards the top of the market were prices found to be much the same and there criticisms of style and quality began to emerge. Purchasing practice was consistent with the views expressed. Towards the upper end of the market, suits were imported because their design was superior or because comparable goods were not available in the United Kingdom. For the rest, imports were purchased on grounds of price alone; if British prices were reduced by 10 per cent most retailers would increase the proportion of purchases from the United Kingdom, though some would require a rather larger reduction to induce a shift from imports. This attitude may well be representative of retailers of a wide range of menswear. It was noticeable that retailers of menswear were generally more critical of British prices and more inclined to import because of price differentials than were retailers of ladieswear and mixed clothing.

WOMEN'S BLOUSES

Initially the development of import penetration in the market for women's blouses was similar to that in men's suits with a jump from 40 to 45 per cent in value and from 42 to 55 per cent in volume between 1980 and 1982. Since then, however, the position has been held with the import ratio fluctuating fairly widely but never surpassing the 1982 level in terms of value and only slightly in terms of volume. It is often suggested that rising demand is bound to be satisfied by imports so it is worth noting that the market for blouses has been rather more buoyant than that for suits.

Again the shift in the ratio of domestic to foreign prices explains the rise in imports and at least in part their comparative stability in recent years. BCIA figures show an increase from 1.77 in 1977 to 2.04 in 1981, rather smaller proportionately than for men's suits, followed by a fall to 1.62 in 1985, which is a very much bigger drop proportionately. It is possible, however, that a more important reason has been the shift in fashion away from very lightweight cotton blouses, which has induced a fall in imports from India. Other low-cost suppliers, mostly in the Far East, have continued to expand sales in this country. Together they account for more than three quarters of imports by volume, over two fifths of consumption. As with suits, unit values suggest that the gap between their prices and domestic products gives them an unassailable advantage.

While the low-cost suppliers have held their ground, quality producers have built up market share rapidly, despite the movement of relative prices against them. Italy, and more recently Germany, sell goods of excellent design and quality. The German success is particularly striking. Despite very high prices the volume of sales more than doubled within two years. It is here that British producers are perhaps most vulnerable to growing import penetration.

In purchasing, retailers emphasise delivery, style, quality and performance, in that order. Price is of less account though it is more important than service from manufacturers, apart from delivery, and almost invariably more important than novelty. Retailers consulted about blouses were all importing directly and most of them also via British manufacturers; comparatively little use was made of other channels. The share of imports in purchases ranged from under 10 to over 40 per cent, but with a fair number of high importers. Supplies originated overwhelmingly in the Far East though there was some buying in Western Europe. More than half of the respondents found British prices higher and nearly half thought British style and quality inferior, while doubts were expressed about product performance, delivery and flexibility of supply. The high importers were much more critical of British goods than the rest. The chief reason for importing was the lack of comparable goods in the United Kingdom, though price and design were also equally important. At the upper end of the market, design was a major reason for importing; in other sectors price was a stronger motive. Several retailers said they would increase the proportion of British goods purchased, if British prices were reduced relative to those of imports and if style and appearance were improved.

KNITWEAR: JUMPERS AND PULLOVERS

Trade in this category of knitwear is similar to that in blouses, with a big import of low-price garments from the Far East, principally knitted from man-made fibres, though wool jerseys are also supplied in quantity, especially from Hong Kong. Import penetration in terms of value rose from 36 per cent of apparent consumption in 1980 to 39 per cent in 1982 and 46 per cent in 1984. It was reduced to 43 per cent in 1985. In volume terms the pattern was similar, the ratio rising from 44 per cent in 1980 to 49 per cent in 1985. These figures are rather higher than in most other knitted goods, though low in comparison with some. Import penetration in knitted shirts, for example, was 81 per cent in terms of value in 1985 and 93 per cent in terms of volume.

Statistics on production and trade in jerseys suggest that here at least prices did not get quite so badly out of hand as in some sectors of non-knit clothing, although the ratio of domestic to import unit values did rise to 1981. It then fell from 1981 to 1984 but moved up again sharply in 1985. United Kingdom prices are perhaps closer to Far Eastern prices than in blouses, but the gap still gives the Far East a strong competitive edge. The Community, which in this context largely means Italy, is increasing its share of the market. The Italians are able to keep costs down because a great deal of production is in the hands of small firms that escape social charges. But the great advantage of the Italian industry lies in its design flair. United Kingdom manufacturers have in the past been reluctant to employ designers. They claimed that the large retailers' insistence on production to specific price points caused them to neglect design innovation. In the last few years this has changed, at least among the larger producers, as has the use of new design and production techno- logies. British producers are investing heavily in new technologies that permit a quicker response to the market, but the benefits are yet to show in trade or in the views of British goods expressed by retailers who replied to questionnaires.

All the retailers asked about knitwear emphasised the importance of style, quality and delivery in purchasing decisions. They were generally regarded as 'very important', with price and product performance close behind. All the respondents were large or very large importers, buying both from Western Europe and the Far East or other low-cost suppliers; and almost all imported directly, though usually supplementing this by dealing with importers and wholesalers. Some imports also came to them through United Kingdom manufacturers. It was found in Chapter 4 that high importers viewed British goods with a jaundiced eye, so the fact that they imported extensively may partly explain the very poor view taken of British goods, almost always more expensive and seriously deficient in style. They were also critical of the quality, performance and novelty of British goods, though this last aspect was of little import- ance to most of them. Retailers at the top end of the market were particu- larly critical of the design of British goods. Apart from delivery, however, where views were mixed, all respondents took on the whole a favourable view of the service provided by United Kingdom manufacturers. Price, design and non-availability were of equal importance as motives for importing, the two latter being especially important at the upper end of the market. A particular reason mentioned was the greater reliability of foreign supplies. There was little inclination to increase the proportion of United Kingdom products in purchases, whatever changes were made to British goods, though relatively lower prices or improvements in style would make some difference. Once committed to importing, buyers often seem to find it hard to envisage a change either in their own practice or in the goods offered by British industry.

In sum, the view taken of British products by retailers replying to questionnaires was broadly similar with regard to women's blouses and knitwear, although the emphasis differed. In both cases, the lack of comparable products in the United Kingdom fostered imports; but prices were too high and design inferior. In men's suits, the major cause of imports was price. In all three, there was a marked tendency for retailers serving the upper end of the market to import on grounds of design and non-availability, while others, particularly at the lower end, were more influenced by price. As a group retailers consulted about specific products rated British prices and design much more unfavourably than did retailers asked about clothing in general (though curiously enough they were better satisfied with the service provided by domestic producers); and it is possible, indeed probable in the case of knitwear where import dependence was unusually high, that the sample was biassed.

It should be added, therefore, that in interviews, including some with retailers who did not wish or were unable to reply to questionnaires, considerable emphasis was laid on the improvements that had been made in the clothing and knitwear industries in recent years. Manufacturers were more market-oriented; design and technology had improved; instead of waiting for guidance from retailers, producers were developing new lines on their own initiative. Some of Britain's clothing manufacturers are now rated as good as any in the world. The fact that several leading retailers of clothing besides Marks and Spencer rely heavily on domestic suppliers speaks for itself. None the less, the impression remains that the industry has some way to go before it can compete on level terms with the major European producers.

6

DOMESTIC ELECTRIC APPLIANCES

The domestic electric appliance industry has a different character from the majority of consumer goods industries. Like the motor industry and consumer electronics, it is an engineering industry where economies of scale in production are very significant, which creates problems unusual among the traditional producers of consumer goods. At the same time, however, it shares many of the problems common to non-engineering consumer goods industries, notably the presence among its customers of very large retailers with substantial market power.

Output covers a wide range of products, both the larger appliances (white goods) such as cookers, refrigerators and freezers, and washing machines and a multiplicity of small appliances including the microwave cooker. The value of total output in 1985 was officially estimated at £1,205 million, against £1,140 million in 1984. As usual, the accuracy of this figure is suspect, as are official data on deliveries. The industry's representative body, the Association of Manufacturers of Domestic Electric Appliances (AMDEA), keeps its own statistical records of deliveries of the larger appliances, which differ substantially from those published by the Business Statistics Office and which are preferred by most people close to the industry, although they are less comprehensive in coverage.

Retail sales of domestic electric appliances including power tools were estimated at £2,396 million at retail selling prices in 1984; they are by far the most important element in the broader domestic appliance category, with sales totalling £2,905 million, that includes gas appliances and lawn mowers. Some of the industry's products may also be included in retailing of 'lighting and minor electrical supplies' with sales estimated to be £560 million in 1984. Statistics of demand and output thus cover rather different categories of goods.

Table 6.1 shows the best available indicator of the growth of demand: an index of real consumers' expenditure on major appliances including, as in the retail statistics, gas appliances. Until 1979, demand followed the common pattern of consumer spending, falling from the 1974 peak and subsequently recovering to a new peak; but the average rate of growth was not exceptional. Since then, however, and with increasing momentum, demand has surged, until in 1985 it far surpassed the growth of

Table 6.1. *Indicators of demand, output and trade in the domestic electric appliance industry*

1980 = 100

	Consumers' expenditure at 1980 prices[a]	Output	Volume of imports[b]	Import penetration %	Trade balance %
1974	90.4	122.2	...	27	−4
1975	81.3	115.8	...	25	−5
1976	84.3	106.8	...	27	−4
1977	79.9	107.8	...	30	−4
		—[c]		—[c]	—[c]
1978	89.2	107.5	94.3	30	−6
1979	100.8	109.4	111.0	30	−11
1980	100.0	100.0	100.0	31	−10
1981	100.0	95.9	112.9	36	−20
1982	107.4	98.1	115.8	38	−23
1983	120.2	114.9	136.8	39	−27
1984	130.3	115.5	135.7	43	−30
1985	140.6	118.3	148.3	45	−32

Sources: AMDEA, and see Appendix 1.
[a] Major appliances, including gas appliances.
[b] Refrigeration and laundry equipment, dishwashers and vacuum cleaners. Series derived from Customs and Excise data published by AMDEA.
[c] Bars denote break in series.

consumer spending in general. In contrast to the demand for most manufactured consumer goods other than consumer electronics, it barely faltered in 1980 and 1981 and the abolition of hire purchase controls in July 1982 gave it an extra boost; while for some new products it has risen without interruption. Thus, during the 1980s, the state of the domestic market as a whole has been unusually favourable to suppliers.

Until fairly recently, producers in the United Kingdom have rarely been able to take advantage of these circumstances. Output was already falling sharply in the mid-1970s. It recovered, to some extent, to 1979 and then fell again to 1981. The cutback in production after 1979 was, however, comparatively modest by the standards of most consumer goods industries and the rise from 1982 onwards was well above average. Even so, production in 1985 still probably fell short of the peak levels of the early 1970s.

Meanwhile, imports have soared. The third column in table 6.1 shows an index of the volume of imports of a range of (mostly mature) products. From 1978 to 1985 it rose by 57 per cent as compared with a rise of 10 per cent in output. The volume of total imports has grown still faster than that of goods covered by the index as the rise in import penetration, already high in the 1970s, indicates; while from 1978 onwards exports fell inexorably, stabilising only around 1983. It is indicative of the

Table 6.2. *Import penetration ratios for selected appliances, 1984*

Imports as per cent of apparent volume of consumption

Dishwashers	100	Automatic washing machines	43
Wet-and-dry vacuum cleaners	100	Vacuum cleaners except wet-and-dry	43[a]
Women's shavers	100	Fridge-freezers	29
Cooker hoods	86	Space heaters	23
Build-in ovens	80	Tumble dryers	8
Build-in hobs	76	Free-standing cookers	8
Liquidisers, food mixers, processors	74	Immersion heaters	6
Irons	64	Storage heaters	1
Freezers	62	Electric blankets	1
Single-door refrigerators	50	Twin-tub washing machines	0
Spin dryers	48	Coffee percolators	0

Source: AMDEA.
[a] 1983.

industry's longstanding weakness that exports as well as imports contributed to the loss of output up to 1979, in contrast to the majority of consumer goods industries. Had exports maintained a constant ratio to output and the small rise in import penetration been contained, production in 1979 would have been some 7 per cent higher than it was. The loss since 1979 has been very much greater, equivalent by 1984 to over 30 per cent of the value of output, of which almost two thirds came from rising import penetration; and the industry's trading situation is now one of the weakest among consumer goods industries.

A great part of the rise in import penetration since 1980 is due to the advent of the microwave, and the lack of United Kingdom production to meet the new demand. If microwave cookers are excluded, import penetration in 1985 was equivalent to 39 rather than 45 per cent of apparent consumption. If other 'new' products were excluded, import penetration would appear still lower, though not as low as in 1980 given the rise in imports of mature products. The level of import penetration is, however, notably higher among new products, many of them not made in this country at all in 1984, the last year for which figures are available. Data for a range of products in terms of volume, rather than value, are set out in table 6.2. Only for such old-fashioned items as twin-tub washing machines, those catering to idiosyncratic British tastes such as electric blankets, or those where an exceptional share of retailing is in the hands of the Electricity Boards, such as free-standing cookers, does import penetration fall to negligible proportions.

Imports of domestic electric appliances originate chiefly in Western Europe which, until the advent of the microwave, accounted for something like 85 per cent of all imports. Except in small appliances, the industry is protected from Far Eastern competitors by heavy transport costs. In the 1950s, all European producers were operating on a small scale, but during the 1960s Italian output for both home and export markets was, with government encouragement and support, growing very rapidly with a consequent reduction in costs.[1] Initially the Italian industry competed only on price at the bottom of the market but its products have steadily improved in quality and performance. Producers in the United Kingdom, meanwhile, failed to achieve commensurate increases in scale, partly because of the uncertainties engendered by stop-go policies. Erratic movements in consumer demand, aggravated by stop-go, were one of the reasons for the high level of import penetration in 1974. With demand stimulated by the Barber boom, imports flooded in. Furthermore, slow growth of the British economy and of household incomes relative to other European producing countries meant that in some product lines demand was deemed too small or too slow-growing to support efficient production, even supposing that other cost problems (notably low productivity leading to high labour costs) could have been solved. Both to provide cheaper models and to widen the range for sale under their own brand name, manufacturers themselves resorted to importing during the 1970s, the British-owned companies as well as the multinationals.

By the latter part of the 1970s, surplus capacity was beginning to emerge in the West European industries and cheap products were starting to come in from Eastern Europe. When United Kingdom demand surged in the 1980s, competition from overseas suppliers for increased market share became intense, leading to severe pressure on prices. It is indicative of this pressure that, whereas from 1974 to 1979 United Kingdom producer prices of domestic electric appliances rose at approximately the same rate as the prices of all non-food manufactures, between 1979 and 1984 they rose less than half as much, by 24.4 per cent against 50.8 per cent. The rise in 1985 of 4.9 per cent was relatively larger, but still below average.

MANUFACTURERS AND RETAILERS

The United Kingdom domestic electric appliances industry is composed of a core of six major firms responsible for the greater part of output of the larger appliances plus smaller specialist firms and producers of small appliances. Three of the majors, Electrolux, Philips and Hoover, are multinationals; the remaining three, Hotpoint, Creda and Thorn, are subsidiaries of major British companies. Concentration has long been and remains high for a consumer goods industry. The five largest enterprises in terms of employment accounted for 53 per cent of sales and work done in 1984; concentration in respect of individual products is very much higher with two or three firms accounting for the bulk of output.

Employment in the industry contracted by almost a third from 1979 to 1983, so that there has been a significant rise in productivity and, in the last few years, the industry has been fighting back vigorously, as witness the recovery in output, although the melancholy tale of plant closures and bankruptcies continues. For example, Philips closed its only British washing machine plant in 1985 on the grounds that it was too small. On the other hand, several new plants are being established by multinational companies including Electrolux, Sharp and Matsushita in microwaves and Kelvinator (Candy) in dishwashers. (Some of their inputs will necessarily be imported, but that would be so whatever the ownership of the plants.) Electrolux has chosen Britain as the base for virtually all its European microwave production partly because there is a large existing market here, bigger than the rest of the European market combined, illustrating the importance of market size. Similar reasoning attracted Japanese investment while Candy decided to restart British dishwasher production because demand has now grown sufficiently to support local manufacture. In many lines, however, the scale of United Kingdom output in total and in terms of individual (British-owned) enterprises remains below the level of its major European competitors; and, of course, there have been changes in Europe too, most importantly the takeover of Zanussi by Electrolux which gives the latter a quarter of the entire West European market for domestic electric appliances. British-owned firms are minnows in comparison.

Small scale is one major problem: the other is relations with the large United Kingdom retailers, which are extremely bad. An unusually high, and growing, proportion of retail sales is in the hands of multiple retailers, who are fiercely price competitive, selling high volumes with a low margin. In the 1976 Retail Enquiry, large multiples accounted for 57 per cent of sales of all electrical and electronic consumer goods. In the 1982 Enquiry their share had risen to 64 per cent; if the figures had been calculated on the same basis as in 1976 it might have been even higher. A comparable figure for 1984 is not available because of the addition to the group of lawn mowers, where independents retail a larger share of trade, but the large multiples' share was probably still greater than in 1982. Further, an unusually high proportion of sales, probably two thirds or more, is in the hands of specialist retailers. The combination of size and specialisation puts the multiple electrical retailers in a very strong position. Market research data indicate that, including the Electricity Boards, they account for three quarters of all sales of some major appliances. Their share of smaller appliance sales falls to around 40 per cent while mail order firms, variety stores and large grocers account for a third or more of sales of such goods.

Retail concentration data, again covering gas appliances and lawn mowers as well as electric appliances, suggest that the five largest enterprises had 42.4 per cent of sales in 1984. Their average purchases would have been of the order of £150 million, giving a ratio of purchases to sales for the five largest retailers and manufacturers of 1.06 (for an explanation of this ratio see Chapter 5). The average purchasing power of the largest retailers is thus greater than the average sales of the largest manufacturers, though not by a wide margin. The ratio could, however, understate the real strength of the retailers in their dealings with manufacturers. Unfortunately, any assessment of relative strengths in terms of the turnover of individual firms is complicated by the fact that the major manufacturers are, as already noted, usually part of a group while all the big specialist retailers except the Electricity Boards are also leading retailers of consumer electronics.

Turnover data relating to domestic electric appliances alone are available for only two important producers in the United Kingdom. The first is Electrolux whose 1983 United Kingdom turnover, including imports, was £198 million. The second is Lec, an independent British-owned firm which specialises in refrigerators and fridge-freezers, which had British sales of £44 million. These figures are consistent with Census of Production data that give the five largest firms, which do not include Lec, average sales of £130 million in that year.

Among retailers, the combined turnover of Curry's and Dixons in 1984, adjusted to a twelve-month basis, exceeded £650 million excluding VAT. The combined Electricity Boards had turnover approaching £400 million, Comet over £300 million, Rumbelows rather less but probably of the order of £200 million to £250 million. A number of other firms are coming up fast, especially MFI in cooker sales (cutting into Electricity Board sales and boosting import penetration in the process) and Harris Queensway whose turnover in electrical goods, negligible in 1983, approached £100 million in 1985. Setting aside Rumbelows, which is owned by Thorn-EMI, and the Electricity Boards, the leaders are all highly competitive, not to say aggressive, retailers, whose total purchases and in some cases purchases of domestic electric appliances exceed the domestic appliance turnover of any manufacturers in the United Kingdom.

The Electricity Boards are a special case because their policy is to buy from companies with a United Kingdom manufacturing base to help 'to maintain capacity for appliance development in the United Kingdom, particularly for cookers and space and water heating appliances' partly because it maintains 'the electricity demand from this sector of industry'; the LEB told the Monopolies Commission that it 'devoted special attention to appliances which increased demand for electricity and improved the load factor, because this contributed to more effective use of capital plant'.[2] Manufacturers accuse other retailers of fostering imports by purchasing cheaper own-brand goods directly from abroad.

There are really two points at issue in relations between manufacturers and retailers: do the big retailers exert undue pressure on manufacturers, and have they raised the level of import penetration above what it would otherwise have been. It is impossible to give a definite answer to the first question. All that can be said is that the structure of the market is such that it would be possible for retailers to squeeze manufacturers and that it is widely believed that they do so. *The Financial Times* (18 July, 1985) once referred to 'the awesome power of British retailers'. The MMC, quoting the views of refrigerator manufacturers, put it more discreetly: 'large retailers had grown in size and importance and in their ability to impose pressure on manufacturers'.[3]

On the second point, it is true that some of the big retailers import own-brand goods, retailed under British-sounding names, from low-price suppliers. (Manufacturers operating in the United Kingdom are said, incidentally, to be reluctant to supply own-brand goods to retailers for fear that they will undercut the prices of virtually identical manufacturer's brands.) It is equally true that the manufacturers themselves are major importers. As noted in Chapter 4, the response to questionnaires and requests for interviews among large retailers was poor, and the replies that were received may not be representative. It is worth pointing out, however, that almost all those who did reply obtained at least some of their imports via manufacturers in the United Kingdom, and several of those who were heavily dependent on imports obtained them exclusively through manufacturers. The only published data on manufacturers' imports relate to small appliances in the mid-1970s, when the Price Commission estimated that United Kingdom manufacturers sold about one third of all imports which then accounted for about 30 per cent of the value of apparent consumption.[4] There are clear traces in the trade figures of importing by foreign multinationals with plants in the United Kingdom (Electrolux from Denmark and Sweden, Philips from the Netherlands) as well as of retailer importing; but it is impossible to deduce how much British-owned manufacturers import. We would guess that, in total, manufacturers operating in the United Kingdom import as much as or more than retailers importing directly on their own account. The real reason for importing rather than purchasing a similar British appliance has been that British products have not been competitive in price nor satisfactory in design; in many cases a similar British appliance has not been available. Manufacturers and retailers import for similar reasons.

With the fall in the pound relative to European currencies and recent changes for the better in United Kingdom industry (it was emphasised in interviews that there have been great improvements since 1982) things may be changing. It is interesting that in the related area of consumer electronics, Dixons, which traditionally sources its television sets in the Far East, has concluded a deal with Thorn-EMI which will mean that it buys in Britain about half the colour TV sets its expects to sell in Britain.

TWO-DOOR FRIDGE-FREEZERS

One of the three products examined in detail was the fridge-freezer, where the development of output and trade has been notably more favourable than in most of the domestic electric appliance industry. It was chosen for this very reason, to discover why, in an industry with a generally poor record on import penetration, fridge-freezers were an exception.

Demand for fridge-freezers, in terms of volume, rose by some 56 per cent between 1978 and 1985, faltering only in 1980 and rising particularly sharply in 1981 and 1982. Output which had built up during the late 1970s showed a continuous and rapid increase, and by 1985 was two and a half times as large as it had been in 1978. As output rose, the unit value of United Kingdom fridge-freezers delivered to the home market relative to the unit value of imports declined, their ratio falling from 1.19 in 1978 to 1.09 in 1980 and 0.91 in 1982. It fluctuated around 1.00 thereafter, rising again to 1.06 in 1985. The volume of imports fell from over 400,000 units in 1978 to less than 270,000 two years later and was fairly close to this level throughout the early 1980s. As a result, the share of imports in supplies to the United Kingdom market fell dramatically, from 68.6 per cent in 1978 to 48 per cent in 1980 and 28.9 per cent in 1984, rising for the first time in many years to 29.7 in 1985. All this is in marked contrast to developments in one-door refrigerators where demand was sluggish, output has fallen, import penetration has risen and the ratio of British to import unit values remains higher than in 1978.

In fridge-freezers producers in the United Kingdom were quick to recognise their opportunity and to adapt their design to British requirements which differ somewhat from Continental tastes. An important reason for the fall in import penetration was Hotpoint's decision to manufacture here rather than buy in from Zanussi, illustrating the critical importance of manufacturers' sourcing policy for trade. In 1983, Hotpoint held 15 per cent of the market for all home refrigeration equipment according to market research estimates; assuming a similar share in fridge-freezers alone, import penetration would have been of the order

Table 6.3. *Imports of two-door fridge-freezers*[a]

	1979		1985		
	'000s	% of value	'000s	% of value	unit value £
Italy	364.3	77.3	217.7	74.7	125.1
Germany	7.1	1.8	11.0	4.9	162.2
Scandinavia[b]	15.1	5.6	30.9	15.5	182.4
Yugoslavia	—	—	5.7	1.5	94.7
Eastern Europe[c]	—	—	8.5	0.4	50.0
Total	436.0	100.0	274.6	100.0	132.7

Source: AMDEA, based on Customs and Excise data.
[a] Figures for 1979 relate to imports by countries of consignment, for 1985 to countries of origin and may not be strictly comparable.
[b] 1979 Denmark only, 1985 Denmark, Sweden and Finland.
[c] USSR, Romania and East Germany.

of 45 per cent rather than below 30 per cent had Hotpoint continued to source in Italy.

Table 6.3 illustrates the pattern and development of trade in fridge-freezers. The Community supplied 85 per cent of imports by value in 1979 and 81 per cent in 1985. Italy still has by far the largest share of the market, but the volume of its sales has fallen by two fifths since 1979. Scandinavia, supplying fridge-freezers of high unit value to supplement the Electrolux range, has gained ground, as has Germany, another quality supplier. At the bottom of the market, Eastern Europe and Yugoslavia, which did not supply fridge-freezers in 1979, had achieved a 2 per cent share by 1985. On the whole, however, competition for appliances of the type made in Britain is restricted to Italian machines, with only a few smaller suppliers, notably Spain, operating in the same price range.

Retailers consulted about fridge-freezers gave the greatest importance to price and delivery in their purchasing decisions, followed by style and appearance, performance and promotion, and by quality. Other purchasing factors, though still important, were less significant. Those retailers who did not do their own servicing laid great emphasis on good after-sales service; otherwise differences appeared to arise from the market sector served, despite the fact that almost all of them claimed to sell to all sectors. Their view of British goods was on the whole favourable. Fridge-freezers made in the United Kingdom were sometimes thought to be more expensive, sometimes cheaper than competing imports but on the whole about the same. In all other respects, British goods and producers were rated as good as or better than the competition, save in style and novelty. In the majority of cases, goods were imported because similar products were not made in the United Kingdom, and improvements in the relative price of British-manufactured products would not have induced retailers to purchase more of them, though they might do so were design improved. Clearly, however, given the pattern of production and trade there is little scope for change. Producers in the United Kingdom have reversed the growth of import penetration because they took the opportunity to exploit a growing market, improved price competitiveness and supplied an acceptable standard product.

VACUUM CLEANERS

The second product examined was the vacuum cleaner, a mature product with some natural protection, because of the British consumer's liking for upright models, though less than is provided to fridge-freezers by high transport costs. This market has been much less expansionary than that for fridge-freezers, with demand almost flat from 1978 to 1983 and output falling sharply. Most production is now in the hands of two multi-nationals, Electrolux and Hoover. Imports and import penetration have surged, the share of imports rising from 14.6 per cent in terms of volume in 1978 to 42.7 per cent in 1983. Developments in more recent years are uncertain, because AMDEA no longer publishes data on British deliveries. However, the Business Monitor series for vacuum cleaners indicates a large rise in output since 1983, in response to the improvement in demand when Hoover and Electrolux introduced new models; while the volume of imports, excluding wet-and-dry cleaners, has fallen, so that import penetration may also have declined.

The increase in imports of wet-and-dry cleaners, until very recently not produced in this country, was one of the reasons for the rise in import penetration. Trade figures do not distinguish between cleaners of different types before 1982, but in that year imported wet-and-dry machines took over 9 per cent of the market, and almost as much in 1983. Excluding wet-and-dry, the share of imports in the latter year was 34.9 per cent rather than 42.7 per cent.

In 1985 France provided 44 per cent of imports by value (excluding imports of mainly battery-operated models and of wet-and-dry cleaners) and other West European producers together accounted for a further 39 per cent, most of them (with the exception of Germany and Denmark) supplying products of rather lower average unit value than France or indeed Britain. The East Europeans play a large role in imports at the bottom end of the market with an 8 per cent share in the value of imports but 13 per cent of their number; it is believed that East European cleaners are imported principally by Mail Order firms. Unfortunately, figures for imports in earlier years are not comparable because of changes in coverage, but it is clear that France has greatly increased its share of the import market and that the number of machines imported from France has risen sharply. This reflects Hoover's decision to switch production of cylinder models to France. In this instance, in contrast to fridge-freezers, a producer's decision on sourcing led to an increase in import penetration over and above what would otherwise have occurred. The German share in imports, 13.3 per cent in 1985, has for once not risen, though some other Community producers have increased their share while the East European share is probably twice as large as in 1979.

The importance given to various buying factors by retailers when purchasing vacuum cleaners differed to a surprising extent from the weight attached to them when purchasing fridge-freezers. Great stress was laid on performance, followed by promotion and quality, then style, novelty, delivery and knowledge of the market, the last four ranking equally. Price was near the bottom of the list. Retailers were also influenced by the market share of different brands, some buying to widen the range, others concentrating on successful brands. Retailers' opinion of vacuum cleaners made in Britain was that they were as good or better than imports, save on novelty. In particular, United Kingdom producers could not supply specialised items, whereas some smallish overseas producers, Goblin for example, had found a niche to exploit. There is, however, at least one small British producer which by 1986 was successfully pursuing a similar policy, making inroads in the wet-and-dry market with a unique, high-priced product. Imports were purchased principally because similar products were not available in the United Kingdom; though design was also mentioned as a reason for importing and improvements in design would encourage some retailers to purchase more in Britain. As with fridge-freezers, however, retailers though satisfied with goods produced in the United Kingdom did not expect to alter their buying habits.

ELECTRIC IRONS

The third product group examined was electric irons. Unfortunately AMDEA statistics no longer cover small electric appliances in detail, and there are serious gaps in the BSO's production statistics; so that the magnitude of changes in output and trade is uncertain. It is clear, however, that output has fallen while imports and import penetration have increased. AMDEA estimates for 1979 suggest that British deliveries to the home market then exceeded two million irons and that the import penetration ratio, in terms of volume, was 30 per cent, though higher in dry irons and lower in the more sophisticated and expensive steam and steam-spray irons. Output fell in 1980 and 1981 and since then appears to have fluctuated around 1.4 million units. Within this total,

Table 6.4. *Imports of electric irons, 1984*

	Dry			Steam, steam-spray and extra steam		
	'000s	% of imports by value	unit value £	'000s	% of imports by value	unit value £
Germany	8.8	2.2	8.86	868.3	47.5	9.46
France	40.4	8.0	7.03	499.7	22.4	7.74
Other EC	44.8	10.2	8.10	488.7	24.0	8.48
Far East[a]	486.6	61.5	4.48	72.5	2.9	6.83
Eastern Europe[b]	166.2	12.5	2.67	65.5	1.2	3.25
Total	763.0	100.0	4.65	2,197.3	100.0	8.50

Source: AMDEA, based on Customs and Excise data.
[a] Dry – Hong Kong, Singapore, Taiwan; steam, etc. – Hong Kong and Singapore.
[b] Dry – East Germany, Czechoslovakia, Poland; steam, etc. – East Germany and Czechoslovakia.

output of dry irons is higher than in 1981 and of steam and other irons lower. AMDEA estimates that imports supplied 63.5 per cent of the market in 1984 and their share would have been still higher in 1985. The volume of imports in that year was three and a half times as large as in 1979, with imports of steam and other irons almost four and a half times as large.

This sector of the industry lacks the natural protection given to the large appliances by high transport costs. As a result, Asian suppliers predominate in imports of dry irons, with unit values on average close to those of British producers. Cheaper models come from Eastern Europe, more expensive, better-quality goods from the rest of the Community, as may be seen from table 6.4. In steam irons and other advanced models the usual trade pattern reappears with the Community being the major supplier. High-quality imports from Germany are of outstanding importance.

The pattern of imports again reflects manufacturers' sourcing decisions as well as retailers' own-brand purchases. Germany's market share in steam, steam-spray and extra steam derives from Rowenta's market share; top-quality Rowenta irons are made in West Germany though some of its dry irons come from East Germany. Tefal irons come from France, Philips principally from the Netherlands; Sunbeam, like Rowenta a subsidiary of Alleghany International, imports from Italy. Of the major British producers Morphy Richards (recently taken over by Glen Dimplex) manufactures dry and steam irons for sale, both under the Morphy Richards label and as retailers' own brands, but TI's Russell Hobbs irons are imported from Italy, as are retailers' own brands.

Retailers asked about the importance of purchasing factors when buying irons gave equal emphasis to price, quality and performance and almost as much to style and appearance. Otherwise, their requirements differed little from those of buyers of vacuum cleaners, except that novelty was less important. Their view of British products was, however, very different. They were cheaper, but otherwise generally inferior. Save in respect of product performance, retailers were very critical of the design of British irons, and they were unhappy about delivery and promotion as well. Both price and non-availability were mentioned as reasons for importing, but the most frequently mentioned cause was design. Although some retailers did say that the style and appearance of British irons had improved lately, they were virtually unanimous in stating that they would increase the proportion of purchases in the United Kingdom if there were further improvement. Improved prices, quality and performance might also induce a higher proportion of purchasing in Britain, but style and appearance were of overriding importance.

In sum, for the larger appliances the level of imports is determined by retailer own-brand importing and by manufacturers' decisions whether to produce here or import, which in turn are shaped by production costs and the size of the market. Britain competes in standard products but the quality end of the market is wide open to imports and there is growing competition in cheaper lines from Eastern Europe and some new producers. There are some encouraging signs that the range of output is being extended to include newer products, but it remains to be seen whether British-owned firms can exploit them in the longer run. For smaller appliances the situation has more in common with non-engineering consumer goods – weaknesses in design, inability to spot specialised openings or reluctance to exploit them. Innovation in small appliances tends to come from overseas. It is symptomatic that specialist continental manufacturers of small appliances such as Rowenta and Moulinex have built up a worldwide market for their branded goods. British suppliers have hitherto failed to deploy their strengths overseas, as well as losing out at home. The impression given in relation to British-owned firms is that they are now managing to match the Italians on price, but that they remain conservative in design and marketing, unable to compete with the European giants on equal terms yet not ready to survive by specialisation.

7

HOUSEHOLD TEXTILES

DEMAND, OUTPUT AND TRADE

The household textile industry produces mainly bed linen, bathroom and kitchen linen and table linen. It is, however, allied to or associated with the soft furnishings industry which raises a number of problems. Much of the statistical information available covers both industries; that pertaining to household textiles alone, of poor quality in any case, is additionally suspect because of problems of definition and overlapping between the two industries. Their markets are increasingly tending to become one market as the fashion for co-ordinates grows: matching quilts, curtains, chair covers, not to mention wallcoverings and now carpets; matching towels and sheets; drying cloths in the same pattern as china and kitchen storage jars, and so on. Household textiles are being replaced by home fashion. It is in fact here that much of the interest of the industry lies, so far as import penetration is concerned; because it is partly by developing along these lines that the industry has built up its defences against import competition.

Table 7.1 illustrates salient developments in demand, output, trade and, so far as is possible, import penetration since the mid-1970s. Household textiles are thought to account for something over half of consumer spending on what is defined in the national income accounts as expenditure on household textiles and soft furnishings. (In 1985 consumer spending on household textiles alone would have been in the region of £700 to £800 million at current prices, including VAT.) In common with expenditure on other household goods, apart from domestic electric appliances, real outlays fell by more than the average for all consumer spending during the recession and have failed to regain the pre-recession level. Exceptionally, there was a slight fall in expenditure during 1984 and 1985 which may have continued into 1986. Despite this unfavourable pattern of demand, output fell by rather less than the average for all consumer goods during the recession; but it has yet to recover to the pre-recession peak, in this respect sharing the experience of other textile industries. The fall in output since 1983 and the rise in import penetration reflects in part the closure of one major producer.

Britain has long been a net importer of household textiles. In 1974, the value of imports was a little more than twice the value of exports

Table 7.1. *Indicators of demand, output and trade in the household textile industry*

1980 = 100

	Consumers' expenditure at 1980 prices[a]	Output[b]	Import penetration %	Trade balance %	Volume of trade (tonnage) Exports	Volume of trade (tonnage) Imports
1975	96.8	115.8	...	...	67.4	70.4
1976	103.8	108.9	...	...	96.7	70.2
1977	99.9	103.7	...	...	110.9	56.8
					—[c]	—[c]
1978	109.0	105.8	23	−7	107.9	72.6
		—[c]				
1979	105.2	108.3	26	−14	116.2	95.8
1980	100.0	100.0	27	−15	100.0	100.0
1981	99.9	97.2	29	−19	83.7	104.8
1982	100.5	96.5	29	−17	89.7	99.0
1983	103.1	106.7	29	−16	86.3	92.0
1984	102.7	99.7	32	−19	83.5	95.0
1985	102.2	96.1	34	−21	97.9	104.5

Sources: See Appendix 1.
[a] Including expenditure on mattresses and soft furnishings.
[b] Including handkerchiefs prior to 1979.
[c] Bars denote break in series.

and their volume over three times as large. Between 1974 and 1977 the trade deficit was sharply reduced, but with the rise in sterling and in United Kingdom prices the trade position rapidly deteriorated. Unfortunately, there are no adequate published indicators of how prices moved. The only producer price index relates to terry cotton towels and unit values of output cannot be calculated on the same basis as trade unit values because units of measurement differ. The best available guide to relative price changes is a comparison of British export unit values with the unit values of imports from the rest of the European Community as it was then constituted. (Differences in the character of exports and total imports invalidate any comparison with the unit value of total imports.) This shows a rise in the ratio of United Kingdom to EC unit values from 0.81 in 1978 to 1.50 in 1981 for cotton bed linen, and from 0.85 to 1.28 for bed linen of other fibres. It is hardly surprising that total export volume fell by more than a quarter from 1979 to 1981, sales of bed linen falling still more steeply. Meanwhile, domestic consumers switched from the more expensive domestic to the cheaper imported product.

As a result, the ratio of the value of imports to apparent consumption rose from 23 per cent in 1978 to 29 per cent in 1981, while the ratio of net imports to supplies nearly trebled, rising from 7 to 19 per cent.

Thereafter the import ratio was held for three years, as imports fell from their 1981 peak, although in 1984 and 1985 the situation began to deteriorate again. Up to 1983, however, the effect of a deterioration in its trading position on the industry was comparatively modest. From 1979 to 1983, the estimated effect of imports on the value of output was a loss of 3.4 per cent but this was partially offset by an increase in the proportion of output exported. Recession and changes in spending habits probably did substantially greater damage than did the growth of import penetration.

MANUFACTURERS AND RETAILERS

As in many another industry, manufacturers initially reacted to the rise in sterling by slashing margins to hold prices; thereafter they cut their losses by reducing output or leaving the market altogether. The Census of Production shows a fall in the number of enterprises classified to the industry of 7 per cent between 1979 and 1983, from 454 to 422, and of 9 per cent in establishments from 494 to 451, while employment was reduced by almost one third between 1979 and 1982, though it recovered slightly in 1983. More recent estimates suggest a smaller loss of jobs. Even so, the figures imply a big rise in productivity, achieved partly by resort to more capital-intensive methods of production. Possibly even more significant for the industry's future is its increasing market-orientation. More and more manufacturers are emphasising colour and design (all the leading producers have their own designers as well as buying in designs) and are developing specialist products with higher value-added. They are actively promoting their own brand names; one estimate puts the share of manufacturers' brands in sales as high as 40 per cent or so, a remarkable figure for an industry of this kind.

The most outstanding examples of the development of home fashion are such designer-led, and strikingly successful, firms as Coloroll and Laura Ashley, but the older-established producers led by Vantona with its Dorma brand have followed suit. The industry has a core of efficient, design-conscious producers. It is a source of strength that many of the leading producers are part of major textile groups – Courtaulds, Coats Patons and Vantona Viyella, Tootal, and Lonrho, which has its own retail network. The Coats–Viyella merger early in 1986 marked a further major step towards the consolidation of the industry, and the emergence of firms which, though operating independently since economies of scale in production are limited, have massive financial backing.

There is also a large number of smaller enterprises, many of them concerned with only one stage in the production of household textiles, such as making up goods from cloth imported and dyed overseas. Some of the enterprises covered by the Census of Production may be engaged in little more than warehousing foreign products, being essentially marketing subsidiaries of overseas firms. No information is available on the share of smaller firms in output, because household textiles are grouped with soft furnishings and canvas goods in the Production Census analysis of size of firms. The only precise information dates back to the product concentration data of 1977 when the five largest producers accounted for 80 per cent of output of towels, 76 per cent of sheets, 68 per cent of bedspreads, 63 per cent of pillow and bolster cases and smaller shares of other products. Concentration may well be appreciably lower now, as some larger firms have contracted or gone out of business; even so, it is probably higher than in many consumer goods industries. But it is noteworthy that despite their strength and size, major producers feel themselves to be smaller than their big retail customers who, they believe, are in a position to pick and choose their suppliers in a highly competitive market and can exert a good deal of pressure on them.

The greater part of manufacturers' sales go directly to retailers, with the larger producers selling both their own brands and supplying retailers' brands under contract at lower prices. The larger retailers, apart from those in the Lonrho group, import directly from overseas suppliers, but they also make use of import merchants to some extent while there is a little importing via United Kingdom manufacturers. Foreign firms are active sellers in the United Kingdom market. Small retailers deal directly with them and with British manufacturers as well as buying from importers and wholesalers, including group wholesalers; but on the evidence of the questionnaires, direct purchasing from domestic and foreign producers is by far the most important channel of distribution for small as well as large retailers.

Retailing follows a different pattern from that in industries already examined, being probably both less concentrated and less specialised. In official statistics the retailing of household textiles is grouped with soft furnishings. The 1984 Retail Enquiry attributes 18.9 per cent of turnover in the group to retailers with a hundred or more outlets, 26.7 per cent to those with ten to ninety-nine outlets, 16.6 per cent to small multiples, who have been losing market share, and 37.8 per cent to single-outlet retailers whose share, though it had fluctuated during the recession, was then probably very close to their share in 1976. In terms of kinds of business, 46 per cent of 1984 retail turnover was accounted for by mixed retailers with 26.5 per cent by large mixed retailers and 15.9 per cent by mail order business. Specialist retailers of household textiles had 34.6 per cent of turnover, the balance being spread over large grocers with 5.5 per cent of turnover, furniture and other household goods retailers, and drapers.

The share of specialists and independents was probably higher in soft furnishings, implying a greater share for multiple retailers in household textiles. An Economist Intelligence Unit estimate, quoted in the Mellor report published in 1983,[1] put the share of department stores in the retail distribution of bed linen at 40 per cent, mail order 20 per cent, variety stores, discount stores, and small household shops 10 per cent each, with the balance split between markets and other outlets, indicating a much bigger share than does the Retail Enquiry for large mixed retailers and a correspondingly smaller one for independents and specialists. It is believed that the multiples have been increasing market share, with Marks and Spencer now one of the largest suppliers, while the department stores have maintained their share and the independents are losing out. The share of manufacturer–retailers is not known but is thought to be small, although in certain sections of the market it could be significant.

The official retail concentration data for household textiles and soft furnishings probably therefore understate the real degree of concentration in the retailing of household textiles. In 1984, the five largest retailers in this sector were credited with 24.9 per cent of turnover, little higher than the figure for 1982 and on the low side as compared with other products studied. Average purchases by the top five would have been in the region of £35 million or more. The Census of Production for 1984 shows that the maximum average sales and work done by the five largest manufacturers of household textiles and soft furnishings did not exceed £39 million. The ratio of purchases to sales (for an explanation of this ratio, see Chapter 5) among large retailers and producers was thus a good deal less unfavourable to the manufacturers than in many consumer goods industries, though it bears out the manufacturers' claim that they are small relative to their major customers for whom household textiles are only a part, not necessarily a large one, of their trade. However, the picture of sales and purchases suggested by the ratio may understate the relative strength of the very largest producers. Vantona's household textile turnover in 1984 approached £150 million, and Tootal's in the previous year was close on half this figure. Unfortunately, no figures of the household textiles turnover of major retailers are available, so that relative size of individual manufacturers and retailers cannot be judged. Relations between manufacturers and retailers are said to be good and the larger retailers consulted took, on the whole, a favourable view of United Kingdom products and producers.

IMPORT COMPETITION: BED LINEN

Competition from imports follows a rather unusual pattern, both in its geographical origin and in its character. At the top end of the market

Table 7.2. *Imports of bed linen*

	Cotton			Other fibres		
	1981	1984	1985	1981	1984	1985
Value of total imports, £mn	26.3	26.6	33.4	19.9	23.8	28.6
Per cent share in value of imports						
EC ten	10.7	11.5	15.9	6.9	11.2	11.2
Portugal	64.6	68.4	59.5	15.8	56.2	55.3
Other	24.7	20.1	24.6	77.3	32.6	33.5
Imports, thousand tonnes						
EC ten	0.6	0.4	0.7	0.3	0.4	0.5
Portugal	4.6	4.3	4.0	0.7	2.2	2.4
Other	2.1	1.5	2.3	4.2	1.6	1.9
Import unit values, £ per kg						
EC ten	4.77	8.39	7.39	4.33	6.67	6.78
Portugal	3.67	4.26	4.92	4.47	6.14	6.55
Other	3.19	3.62	3.63	3.63	4.99	5.09

Sources: See Appendix 1.

there are relatively small imports of high-priced, high-quality goods from Western Europe, competing principally on design. At the bottom of the market, imports of cheap goods of poor quality come mainly from Asia, especially in toilet and kitchen linen, cleaning cloths and the like. But the chief source of imports is Portugal, which competes mainly, though not exclusively, in standardised middle to lower market goods at very competitive prices. Portugal is a low-labour cost producer with wages comparable to or lower than those of the major Far Eastern clothing exporters. Investment has been high and the industry is well-equipped, while the long-standing historical connection between Portugal and Britain and its privileged position as a member of EFTA have enabled it to establish close links with British distributors. Britain is its chief market while Spain, a potential rival, sells mainly to other European countries, though this could change now that both are members of the EC. At one time Portugal supplied cotton goods almost entirely, but it is increasing the proportion of goods of other fabrics, including mixtures, in its exports, following the shift in consumer demand.

The pattern of imports is illustrated in table 7.2 which covers bed linen. This accounts for around two fifths by value of all imports of household textiles, implying that import penetration is lower than for the industry as a whole. The table gives figures for the peak import year of 1981 when 12,518 tonnes was imported, as well as for 1984 and 1985 when imports totalled 11,784 tonnes. The older members of the Community have acquired a higher import share than in 1981 but it is still modest. The only other significant supplier of high-quality goods is Sweden. Portugal is now the leading supplier of both cotton and other bed linen. Its price advantage over the original members of the Community, as well as domestic producers, is clear in cotton bed linen, as is the still lower import unit value of goods from other sources. In bed linen of other fibres the United States was by far the biggest source of cheap imports in 1981; but as the dollar rose sales melted, chiefly to the benefit of Portugal, despite its apparently smaller price advantage in this sector. Other important sources of supply are Israel, Turkey and Spain with prices rather lower than those of Portugal.

The large volume of imports of cotton bed linen possibly reflects a higher degree of import penetration in the non-retail market (the hotel trade, hospitals and other institutions) than in the retail market. The normal pattern of import penetration is reversed because the non-retail market accepts a more standardised product than the consumer, and possibly also because of its access to large-scale laundry facilities. It is here that the major closure referred to above has affected the market.

Retailers consulted about bed linen, who covered the full range of import dependence from very low to very high, confirmed the great importance attached to design in this industry. Almost all the large retailers rated style and appearance very important; most of them also rated quality very important though they attributed rather less importance to performance and, in general, little to novelty. Price was usually regarded as important; only a minority of respondents considered it very important. Oddly enough, delivery ranked next to style and appearance and ahead of any other purchasing factor, while close contact with suppliers was also rated highly. In comparison with imported products British goods came out very well, being as good or better on all counts. More than half the retailers consulted found the style and appearance of British goods better than foreign; and though they were less enthusiastic about quality and performance, no respondent found British goods inferior to imports in design. They were less happy with some aspects of the service supplied by British manufacturers; delivery and flexibility of supply were sometimes judged inferior to the competition. However, price is a major problem; almost three-quarters of the large retailers found British prices higher than those of imported goods.

Small retailers selling household textiles, clothing and other goods took a similar view on price but were more worried about delivery and were not wholly satisfied as to quality, style and novelty, but it is only fair to add that three of them dealing principally or exclusively in household textiles did not share this dissatisfaction. The most serious criticism of the industry is that, as one retailer put it: 'it fails to spot its opportunities'. Producers go for safety rather than originality and follow the leader (in this case Dorma), all developing the same kind of approach to the market, an attitude that is common among retailers also. As in other industries, foreign firms tend to specialise more and are strong over a narrow range.

Almost all the larger retailers quoted price as a reason for importing, more than half of them referred to non-availability, a few to design and, exceptionally, to the greater ease of dealing with foreign suppliers. It was striking that in an area where design is becoming increasingly important, so few retailers mentioned superior foreign design and quality as a reason for importing, though some others did say they would buy more British goods if design were improved yet further. The comment that it is easier to deal with foreign suppliers may reflect some retailers' dislike of the marketing of coordinated lines, which means higher prices to the retailer and limits his choice. Non-availability refers both to specialised products that would not in any case be produced in the United Kingdom and to goods that could be, indeed have been, produced here but that are no longer available because product lines have been eliminated to reduce costs. This may seem to contradict the comment that British firms are less specialised than their competitors, but it stems rather from the industry's tendency to follow the leader. There is a clear division of opinion between those at the upper and lower ends of the market. At the bottom retailers are happy with style, but dissatisfied with price and to some extent service. Further up market, prices are fairly competitive but design is deficient, which promotes imports in this sector. The overriding reason for importing remains the price of British relative to foreign, specifically Portuguese, products. If relative United Kingdom prices were reduced by 10 per cent or more, almost all the United Kingdom retailers consulted would purchase more British goods.

The household textiles industry has weathered the storms of recent years in remarkably good shape, having achieved an enviable record on design and marketing, and thereby helped to limit the growth of import penetration. Although price remains a problem, it has not been neglected. Earlier on the rise of United Kingdom export unit values against the unit value of imports from the Community was quoted in illustration of the industry's loss of price competitiveness from 1978 to 1981. Between 1981 and 1984, the ratio fell from 1.15 to 0.64 for cotton bed linen and from 1.28 to 0.98 for other bed linen. It rose again in 1985 to 0.84 and 1.03, which is rather less favourable than in 1978; but this probably reflects improvements in the product rather than any real loss of price competitiveness. With the decline in sterling against the major European currencies, the United Kingdom industry may now have the opportunity to exploit its strength in export markets and to contain import penetration.

8

FURNITURE

The furniture industry is variously defined in different sources. In official production statistics, 'furniture' relates to upholstered and wooden furniture for domestic and office use, other wooden cabinet work, beds and mattresses. Metal furniture of all kinds is classed as a separate industry. Total output of the latter in 1984 was estimated to be £456 million, of which only a fraction is domestic furniture. Output of wooden and upholstered furniture was very much larger, estimated at £2,221 million in 1984. Detailed statistics cover only some 70 per cent of output and employment in the industry, so that the accuracy of this figure is very suspect. (This industry too is very critical of official statistics.) Among firms covered by regular production enquiries, 70 per cent of 1984 deliveries were finished domestic furniture, composed of 23 per cent upholstered furniture (which may include some office furniture), 23 per cent kitchen furniture, 14 per cent bedroom furniture and the remainder dining room/living room, occasional and unspecified furniture. The composition of total output is unknown because of the missing 30 per cent for which production details are not available. In the same year, consumer spending on furniture and related products was £2,812 million, of which perhaps 85 per cent was furniture. Retail sales of furniture alone were estimated at £2,428 million, including VAT.

Until 1979, the industry was doing comparatively well as the figures in table 8.1 indicate. Demand was relatively brisk, falling only in 1977 and 1978, with consumer spending rising more than outlays on most goods between 1974 and 1979. Output responded with growth way ahead of the majority of consumer goods industries. Import penetration, relatively low in 1974, remained more or less constant until 1978 although there was some deterioration in the balance of trade with a small surplus being converted into a deficit. Exports have never accounted for more than a fraction of output (around 10 per cent): the most important are reproduction furniture sold chiefly in English-speaking countries. From 1979 on, however, the situation altered radically. Demand fell in 1980 and has never recovered to its previous peak. Spending has been diverted to other goods whose prices have risen less rapidly or not at all, and especially of course to electronic consumer goods. Output fell by almost

Table 8.1. *Indicators of demand, output and trade in wooden and upholstered furniture*

1980 = 100

	Consumers' expenditure at 1980 prices[a]	Output	Furniture deliveries at constant 1980 prices	Volumes of imports (tonnage)[b]	Import penetration %	Trade balance %
1974	86.4	101.4	...	...	8	0
1975	91.3	109.9	...	...	7	+ 1
1976	97.3	111.0	...	...	8	+ 1
1977	90.9	109.5	...	...	8	+ 3
		—[c]			—[c]	—[c]
1978	93.9	118.5	...	...	9	− 1
1979	106.2	120.6	...	...	10	− 4
1980	100.0	100.0	100	100	12	− 4
1981	99.0	89.8	91	103	15	− 9
1982	100.7	84.0	84	109	16	− 9
1983	103.3	87.6	88	126	17	−11
1984	101.1	86.9	85	150	18	−12
1985	102.8	89.8	87	168	18	−11

Sources: See Appendix 1.
[a] Including expenditure on mattresses, perambulators, pictures and second-hand furniture.
[b] Chairs and wooden furniture.
[c] Bars denote break in series.

a third between 1979 and 1982, the decline being one of the largest experienced by any consumer goods industry; the recovery since then has been modest. The volume of imports and import penetration rose sharply, as did the trade deficit, though in absolute terms import penetration is still relatively low for a consumer goods industry because of the natural protection afforded by the weight and bulk of the product.

Precise information on how different categories of furniture have been affected is not available; but from data on deliveries by larger firms, deflated by the relevant producer price indices, it appears that the brunt of the decline has been borne by dining room/living room furniture and to a lesser extent upholstered furniture; output of kitchen furniture is now higher than it was and production of bedroom furniture is catching up. This reflects in large part the pattern of demand rather than competition from imports. Import penetration, again calculated from incomplete data, rose at a similar rate in kitchen and dining room/living room furniture, the most and least successful sectors in terms of output. For the industry as a whole, changes in import penetration and net exports were equivalent to a loss of some 10 per cent of output between 1979 and 1984 which is small by the standards of many consumer goods industries, though four times the size of the shift during 1974–9. Almost the whole of it was due to import penetration.

MANUFACTURERS AND RETAILERS

Discussion of the furniture industry is apt to provoke a half-amused exasperation and comments such as: 'it's a cottage industry'; production techniques are 'back in the dark ages'. Indeed, the industry appears to exemplify many of the characteristic weaknesses of British manufacturing – ill-organised, amateurish in management, production rather than market-oriented, lacking marketing and design expertise, undercapitalised and ill-equipped. For this, the structure of the industry is a good deal to blame.

Most of the firms in the industry are small or very small. Precise information is lacking because in the Census of Production data on firm size firms classified to the furniture industry are grouped with shop-fitters. Only eighteen enterprises in the group employed 500 or more in 1984, 169 between 100 and 499, and the remaining 5,639 fewer than 100. These small firms account for a rising share of employment and output, close on 50 per cent of the total in 1984, and their average turnover was less than £250,000. Average turnover in the middle group was not much over £5 million and for the 18 larger firms just over £31 million. These figures may slightly exaggerate the small firm's role in the furniture industry, since it appears that the 25 per cent or so of the group that are shop-fitters are characterised by still greater predominance of the small firm. Even so, it is clear that the typical furniture producer is small to medium-sized.

In itself this is no problem since economies of scale in production are rapidly exhausted. It is reckoned that the upper limit to the turnover of an efficient establishment in the United Kingdom is as little as £3 million in upholstery and up to £30 million for wood and board products, after allowing for buying in of parts; and small continental firms operate successfully. They, however, are reported to be not only much more professionally managed, with greater technical and financial resources, but also more specialised. It is true also that there are many small British producers, virtually craft workshops, successfully producing furniture of excellent quality and design. But the typical firm is family owned and run, providing an occupation and an income for the owner. Because margins are low and financial resources limited, investment is low; selling is done through agents because the firms are too small to employ their own staff. Unlike German manufacturers they will not cooperate in selling; they tend to look at the local competition down the road, rather than the wider market situation. After the beating they took in the recession, there is little confidence in the future.

Between 1979 and 1982 the number of enterprises classified to the furniture industry fell from 3,391 to 3,262 and the number of establishments

Table 8.2. *Furniture purchases by type of store*

Per cent

	1977	1978	1984		1977	1978	1984
Furniture shops:				*Others*:			
Discount/warehouses	12	19	28	Department stores	13	10	9
Multiples	} 40	22	12	Mail order	9	5	6
Independents		25	20	Builders merchants/DIY	...	3	5
Specialists	...	2	5	All other	...	14	15

Source: FIRA.

rather more. Though large in absolute terms, this was a proportionately smaller fall than in most consumer goods industries, and because entry is easy, the numbers began to pick up again in 1983 and have probably risen further since then. The recession bore most heavily on the medium to large firms. Several of them went bankrupt; others cut back on employment and output, or shifted to the contract market where there are many small outlets and price is a less important factor. In the industry as a whole, employment fell by 24 per cent between 1979 and 1983 to 78,000, and labour productivity rose by over 20 per cent. A side effect of the recession was to reduce the level of concentration, already exceptionally low. For furniture and shop fitting together, the five largest enterprises accounted for a mere 8 per cent of sales in 1984; if all these were furniture producers, which they probably were, their share in the industry's sales was not much over 10 per cent.

Concentration in furniture retailing, by contrast, is rising fast. The 1982 Retail Enquiry put the share of the five largest enterprises in the retailing of furniture and floor coverings other than carpets at 25.8 per cent; the 1984 figure for a slightly wider range of goods, including perambulators, nursery furniture, prints and picture frames, where retail concentration is very low, was 32.2 per cent. The average turnover of the five largest retailers was £170 million including VAT; the ratio of their estimated average purchases to the sales of the five largest manufacturing enterprises was about 2.3 (for an explanation of this ratio, see Chapter 5) – the highest of any calculated outside clothing and knitwear. An unusually high proportion of retailing, around two thirds, is in the hands of specialists in furniture and related products; and all the major retailers are specialists.

A clearer picture of developments in retailing than is provided by the Retail Enquiry comes from the regular sample surveys of furniture purchases made by the Furniture Industry Research Association (FIRA), which are summarised in table 8.2. The large warehouse-type operators are sweeping all before them. Initially they cut into the market share

of department stores and mail order firms; latterly they have been squeez-
ing the traditional high street multiples such as Waring and Gillow and
the independents. The only other groups to increase their market share
are such specialist firms as Sharps which retails fitted bedroom furniture,
firms selling direct to the public which in 1984 had 2 per cent of the
market, and the big DIY stores. The latter operate mainly in the self-
assembly market as does MFI, the biggest warehouse operator, whose
share of self-assembly products is approaching 50 per cent. In total furniture sales, however, it has been overtaken by Harris Queensway which
operates both warehouses and multiples. Harris Queensway's total turnover, excluding VAT, was £370 million in 1984, of which its furniture
stores (including the joint operation with Debenhams) accounted for
£203 million. The deal with GUS mentioned in Chapter 3 could add
a further £100 million or so initially. MFI's (more specialised) turnover
was equivalent to some £328 million in 1984. The largest British manufacturer, Christie Tyler, had total turnover of £83 million in 1983/4. No
other publicly quoted British furniture manufacturer had turnover in
excess of £40 million.

   The difference in the size and financial strength of retailers and manufacturers has soured relations between them. Retailers dictate prices;
as in other consumer goods industries, manufacturers complain bitterly
that retailers exploit their market power to squeeze producers' margins.
For retailers there is great difficulty in securing supplies from domestic
producers in sufficient quantities – or at all. The director of Marks and
Spencer's home furnishings division is reported to have said of the furniture manufacturers who might have supplied their new stores: 'they beat
a path away from our door'.[1] Communication between the two sides
is hindered by the fragmented nature of the industry and by secretiveness,
while neither side understands the other's difficulties. Delivery is a peren-
nial problem. Wholesaling is and always has been unimportant in this
trade, accounting for less than 5 per cent of deliveries, because of the
space it would require and the risk of damage, so that most production
is to order with deliveries direct to the retailer. One retailer commented
that manufacturers quoted delivery dates that they could not physically
meet from existing capacity – powerful evidence of the amateurishness
of management.

   If manufacturing is backward, so too is a good deal of retailing other
than the retailing of self-assembly furniture. MFI spotted a gap in the
market that conventional retailers were unable to supply. The growth
of demand for fitted kitchen furniture probably owes a good deal to
its operations. Otherwise the kind of sophisticated, selective approach
to the customer that has transformed other retail sectors is only now
beginning to develop. Hitherto, there has been fierce competition among

the major retailers on price, with the rest trailing. Independent retailers have a poor reputation: 'a pretty primitive trade, staffed by people with little real knowledge of what they are selling'. (The fact that specialist furniture retailers abroad were better qualified than they are in this country was mentioned as helping overseas producers.) The Habitat operation has been almost unique in its emphasis on design and style, apart from some small, highly specialised and very expensive shops. All this is changing. Potentially the most important development is Marks and Spencer's entry into the market on a large scale with the creation of specialised satellite stores, selling a coordinated range of furniture and furnishings. Next has also broadened its range with the launch of Next Interior, again supplying coordinates, and others may follow suit. Harris Queensway and other traditional retailers are sprucing up their stores, to make furniture purchasing a more agreeable undertaking. On the manufacturer's side, the specialists as already noted are developing their own outlets and direct selling, while some of the larger firms are attempting to create brand-consciousness among consumers, at present almost non-existent, and are establishing their own shops and exclusive franchises. Manufacturer-owned outlets may now account for between 12 and 15 per cent of the market, and their share is increasing. Finally, a new Furniture EDC has been established which may persuade retailers and manufacturers to communicate more freely. It has already promoted one 'Better Made in Britain' exhibition, hoping to check or reverse the flooding tide of imports.

Whether the industry will be able to take advantage of these developments is doubtful, apart from a handful of manufacturers already committed to greater investment in design and to more active marketing. The growing emphasis on selling coordinates will expose still further what is widely regarded as one of the industry's most serious weaknesses. Retailers argue that furniture is a fashion trade so that style and colour are all-important and complain of the lack of originality in British design. Manufacturers retort on the retailers that they are providing what the public wants. Designers criticise both and are themselves criticised for their lack of understanding of market requirements and business methods. All of them complain that the British consumer is reluctant to spend on furniture, apart from built-in furniture that will enhance the value of a house. It is frequently, and perhaps justly, pointed out that spending per head on furniture in this country is lower than in many others in Europe, as is apparent from data published by FIRA in 'The Furniture Industry in Western Europe'. The validity of such comparisons, based on expenditure converted to a common currency by official exchange rates and ignoring income differences, may be doubted. A more telling comment was made by a retailer who said that customers were prepared

Table 8.3. *Origins of furniture imports, 1984*

	Wood-frame upholstered	Other chairs of wood	Bedroom	Dining room/ living room	Kitchen	Parts of wood
Total imports, £mn	56.7	16.5	40.9	74.6	106.6	44.4
% of total:						
EC	58.6	26.6	58.2	51.9	91.7	58.1
of which: Germany	6.0	2.4	26.4	7.0	66.8	15.1
Italy	20.6	15.8	6.8	14.6	4.7	11.5
Denmark	6.7	1.2	11.0	14.5	0.8	10.8
EFTA	9.9	1.8	8.1	5.8	0.6	7.7
E. Europe	22.6	26.7	21.0	20.2	4.3	1.4
Other	8.9	44.9	14.0	22.1	3.4	32.8

Source: FIRA.

to spend only as much on a chair or a sofa as they would spend on a suit. He considered that warehouse operations had conditioned the public to expect low prices for furniture.

IMPORTS: DINING ROOM/LIVING ROOM FURNITURE

In the light of the growth and pattern of imports the argument that consumers are not prepared to spend is not wholly convincing. The pattern of trade in the most important categories of upholstered and wooden domestic furniture is shown in table 8.3. (Some of the furniture included under these heads may not, in fact, be imported for the household market; there is no way of distinguishing between, for example, chairs imported for office use and those for the home.) The Community supplies about two thirds of the total of items listed, as it does of the wider category of 'all furniture', but its share varies considerably from one sector to another. Germany dominates the kitchen furniture market, supplying fitted kitchen furniture of very high quality; Italy is the leading supplier of upholstered furniture, particularly the fashionable leather-covered sofas and chairs, as well as of non-upholstered chairs, and with Denmark is an important source of dining room/living room furniture. The EFTA countries too, principally Sweden, are important in some sectors. Thus something like three quarters of all imports are goods of high quality and design, with correspondingly high prices. At the other end of the market are cheap, possibly dumped, goods from Eastern Europe and there is an increasing volume of imports from the Far East, especially Taiwan, of (again) cheap and usually self-assembly furniture.

In the industries previously studied, imports from Eastern Europe appeared to be purchased very largely by the big retailers. Although they do import directly from low-price sources, the pattern for furniture may be rather different. A high proportion of imports is handled by United Kingdom manufacturers who import goods at various stages of completion and sell them as their own. This is particularly the case for chairs, which may be bought to supplement a range and can be polished and finished to match domestically-produced tables; this practice is believed to be widespread at the lower end of the market. In fact it appears that manufacturers are larger importers than retailers. A FIRA survey of import channels in 1984, covering 87 per cent by value of wood furniture imports, put manufacturers' imports of finished products at 22 per cent of the total whereas retailers' imports accounted for only 16 per cent. A further 21 per cent of imports, covering semi-finished parts and components, was handled by manufacturers and DIY firms. The remainder consisted of finished products handled by overseas firms exporting to the United Kingdom market and their agents.

When asked about the importance of various purchasing factors in relation to dining room/living room furniture, large retailers put delivery at the top of the list, rating it very important almost without exception. This may merely reflect the fact that furniture, because of its bulk, is difficult to hold in stock but it could also be a reaction to the shortcomings of British producers. Quality ranked next, closely followed by style, both again very important to a majority of retailers. Price came fourth with less than half of all respondents rating it very important. Product performance, close contact with suppliers and flexibility in supply were generally rated important, occasionally very important; knowledge of the market was judged to be important on average but promotion and novelty were little regarded.

Most retailers consulted were low importers, though import dependence tended to be higher at the top end of the market. Nearly all of them imported directly; almost as many used import merchants and purchased some foreign goods via manufacturers. Imports came principally from Western Europe as might be expected, but some purchases were made in Eastern Europe and the Far East or occasionally elsewhere. Compared with foreign suppliers, British manufacturers came down badly on delivery and price. British products were generally judged to be as good as or better than imported furniture on style and quality although, as usual, retailers at the top end of the market found British prices more competitive and were less happy on style than were others. There was no difference, however, in their assessment of quality. The prime reason for importing was that comparable goods were not available in the United Kingdom; price was a close second. Design and the difficulty of dealing with United Kingdom suppliers were mentioned by retailers at the top end of the market, who also imported to secure exclusivity and commented on the more comprehensive ranges available from

European sources. The small retailers are less concerned about price. They import to achieve exclusivity, because of the consumer appeal of foreign products, because United Kingdom delivery is bad, because foreign quality control is better, and (again) because United Kingdom producers are reluctant to expand output to meet demand.

Retailers professed a striking readiness to increase the proportion of British furniture in their purchases if style and appearance were improved. This was perhaps the best indicator of their dissatisfaction with the industry, tending to contradict the fairly good opinion of the design of British goods expressed in reply to questionnaires. About half of them said they would import less if quality and performance were improved and also if relative prices were reduced. Since large retailers attach importance to price, sterling's fall against continental currencies may bring some easing of the pressure of import competition. Even so, it is generally believed that import penetration will continue to increase. Short of a transformation of the industry, there is nothing to prevent it doing so.

9

TOILETRIES; CHINA; WALLCOVERINGS

In this chapter, we look at three industries with comparatively low import penetration that are also net exporters – cosmetics and toiletries, domestic china and earthenware, and wallcoverings. The development of import penetration and of the balance of trade for all three is shown in table 9.1. All of them started from a relatively strong position and have experienced some deterioration in their trading position, but in none of them has import penetration risen as fast as in consumer goods industries on average, while the balance of trade in relation to supplies deteriorated by less than the average save in the case of china and earthenware after 1979. In wall coverings, the deterioration was close to the average. It appears that this and the china industry may have sacrificed exports partly to resist import penetration, as so many other industries did in earlier years.

COSMETICS AND TOILETRIES

This is the only one of the three industries for which adequate indicators of demand and output are available, and for the latter they go back only to 1979. Real consumer spending on toiletries and associated products (toilet soap, paper products and accessories produced by other industries) was sluggish in the late 1970s. It fell sharply after 1974 and remained unusually slack until 1979, when it was still 4 per cent below the 1974 level. Since then, it has risen roughly in line with total consumer spending, picking up sharply in 1984 and 1985. The recession affected output much less than in other consumer goods industries; it fell by only 5 per cent between 1979 and 1982, although employment was cut back very sharply, by almost a quarter from 1979 to 1983. As demand rose so did output; by 1985 it was almost 30 per cent higher than in 1979. These data are hard to reconcile with the industry's own view that demand is more or less saturated and that output has grown slowly. It appears that the official figures reflect a very large estimated increase in the output of small firms and some diversification into other products by firms classified to the industry. They may also give greater weight to the emergence of new products. Changes in hair styles have led to a boom in sales and production of hair care products and rising incomes have promoted demand for luxuries, even though such commodity-type products as toothpaste may have been largely unaffected.

Table 9.1. *Import penetration and the balance of trade in three successful industries*

Per cent

	Cosmetics and toiletries		Domestic china and earthenware		Wall coverings	
	Import penetration	Trade balance	Import penetration	Trade balance	Import penetration	Trade balance
1974	8	+8	17^a	$+32^a$	5^a	$+29^a$
1975	7	+8	...	...	...	...
1976	8	+11	...	...	...	...
1977	10	+16	...	...	...	...
	$—^b$	$—^b$				
1978	10	+15	...	...	6	+31
1979	13	+12	22^a	$+34^a$	6	+30
1980	12	+14	...	...	7	+31
1981	12	+12	...	...	6	+24
1982	13	+11	...	...	8	+25
1983	15	+11	...	...	9	+24
1984	17	+11	24^a	$+20^a$	9	+22
1985	18	+10	...	...	11	+22

Source: See Appendix 1.
[a] Estimated.
[b] Break in series.

Imports come almost entirely from the rest of the Community and thence mainly from France. Of the 81 per cent of imports by value supplied by the EC in 1985, France alone provided 56 per cent. Germany is the next largest supplier with a 17 per cent share of imports in 1985; it has been gaining share steadily over the past decade. (Surprisingly, despite a further rise in the Community's share in 1986, both Germany and France lost ground.) The only major non-Community supplier is the United States, whose share of imports has fluctuated between 10 and 15 per cent. French predominance is principally due to the demand for French perfume – a unique product. It provides a perfect illustration of the lack of comparable United Kingdom products being the reason for imports. It has also been the cause of most of the rise in import penetration since 1979; if the increase in perfume imports between 1979 and 1985 is excluded, the import penetration ratio rises from 13 to only 14 per cent, while the trade balance relative to supplies would have improved from 12 to 14 per cent.

There are several unusual features in the industry's structure. Separate figures relating to toiletries enterprises are not published in the Census of Production but it seems probable that, although small firms account for at least 15 per cent of deliveries, the industry is characterised by relatively large enterprises and a degree of concentration higher than is common in consumer goods industries. It is also fairly heavily populated by multinational enterprises, offshoots either of very large, chiefly American,[1] producers of toiletries or of firms engaged in related activities including such British firms as Beechams and Unilever. (It may be too that its close connections with the chemical industry are a source of strength.) Among the leading producers there are several with turnover in the range of £50 million to £100 million such as Colgate-Palmolive and Elida Gibbs (a Unilever subsidiary) in toiletries and Avon in cosmetics, besides a number with turnover of more than £20 million. Uniquely, the largest retailer, Boots, is also a major manufacturer. Although retailers own brands are gaining market share, manufacturers' brands remain strong in toiletries and still more in cosmetics, where the customer may be paying as much for the name and the package as for the product itself. All the larger firms have their own marketing departments and spend heavily on advertising and promotion. Product changes are frequent, and the launch of a new product will soon be followed by rival firms. They have been quick to spot emerging changes in demand and react. For producers in the United Kingdom, hair care preparations have been the most buoyant sector of the market. Deliveries by firms with more than 25 employees more than doubled in value between 1979 and 1985, while exports rose still faster. In real terms, of course, the rise was very much less, but what is striking is that the growth of deliveries of new products regularly outpaced that of established goods. At the same time, the strength of the larger firms has meant that smaller producers have been forced to find a niche for themselves, often exploiting the cosy, rural picture of England as an aid to selling, as do Woods of Windsor. Their ability to expand tends, however, to be limited by the threat of takeover or the use of successful innovations and ideas by the big firms. Only Body Shop has escaped from this dilemma, with a very distinctive and specialised range of products, and its own chain of shops.

Almost three quarters of all retail sales were handled by food stores and mixed retailers in 1984, with the five largest retailers having 42.5 per cent of the market and average turnover of £184 million. These figures are, however, rather misleading, both because toiletries and cosmetics have different patterns of distribution and because one retailer dominates both sectors. Boots is generally credited with around one third of all sales. In toiletries and associated products, food retailers, especially the large supermarket chains, have a combined share close to that of Boots, but in cosmetics their share is only one fifth or thereabouts and confined to the lower price end of the market. Door-to-door selling is responsible for a similar share of cosmetic trade; Avon, the largest producer, uses

this method of selling. The rest of the market is shared between a variety
of outlets: department stores, independent chemists, drugstores and
others. A recent development is the addition of cosmetics and toiletries
to the range of goods sold by such life-style retailers as Next.

Collectively, however, the market is dominated by very large retailers.
In 1984, single-outlet retailers and small multiples handled a quarter
of retail sales, multiples with 10 to 99 outlets 15 per cent, and the largest
multiples almost 60 per cent. The predominance of the large retailer
does create problems for manufacturers but, as shown above, they themselves include a number of sizeable firms and parts of very large enterprises, so that the respective strengths of manufacturers and retailers
are probably more nearly equal than in other non-food consumer goods
markets. Furthermore, the smaller producers and specialists can distri-
bute through independents and department stores, as well as some specialist multiples. Wholesaling and retail buying groups remain important
for chemists goods, which may further assist the smaller producer.

Retailers expressed an agreeably favourable view of British products
and producers. Save in one instance, they were regarded as being as
good as or better in almost every respect than the competition, and
even the one dissenting respondent did not rely heavily on imports. The
industry was generally found competitive on price and service, even on
delivery. All the same, price was mentioned as often as lack of comparable
products as a reason for importing. The extent to which British goods
are competitive on price varies widely between products; the difference
between British and imported goods is generally smaller on higher-priced
than on commodity-type products.[2] Despite reservations about the style
and quality of British goods, design did not figure among reasons for
importing.

Criticism of design factors refers principally to peripheral goods, gift
toiletries and the like. Foreign suppliers, often very small, were said
to be more specialised, better at niche marketing, more innovative, more
aggressive in seeking markets and readier to adapt their products to
customers' ideas. United Kingdom firms are still too often production-
led, conservative, asking for ideas rather than proposing products. Marketing strategies may be ill-conceived and inflexible. Indeed, by the time
the list of criticisms has been worked through, toiletries begin to sound
like any other British industry rather than a success story. This is perhaps
an exaggeration, but it is clear that it does share some of the weaknesses
of British industry generally.

Import penetration has been limited by a combination of competitive
prices and product innovation. (As pointed out earlier, if trade in French
perfume is excluded, there has been a negligible increase in the import
ratio and the trade balance relative to supplies has improved.) The prime

reason for this success appears to be the presence of a number of sizeable, vigorous and competitive firms whose strength relative to their retail customers is more considerable than is the case in any of the industries previously examined. The industry has benefited from the presence of multinationals, particularly since they export from the United Kingdom. Other factors that could be important are the strength of manufacturers' brands, and the fact that the dominant retailer is also a manufacturer with a foot in both camps. It is these characteristics that have enabled the industry to keep prices competitive and respond to new opportunities rather than the other way about.

DOMESTIC CHINA AND EARTHENWARE

Domestic china is now almost unique among British consumer goods industries. A large part of output consists of high-quality products of traditional design that are characteristically English and have a world-wide reputation. As a result, the industry is still a major exporter, with about half of its output sold overseas, although as the decline in the trade surplus relative to supplies shows, it has lost ground in export markets.

Little reliable information is available on the development of demand and output since figures for the volume of domestic deliveries are not available, and the industry is grouped with other ceramic goods in production statistics and with domestic glassware and hardware in consumption. If domestic deliveries by firms employing 50 or more are deflated by the producer price index to give an estimate of the volume of home sales and combined with data on the volume of trade, it appears that both output and domestic demand remain below the 1980 level though they have recovered from the 1982 low point, and that, remarkably, import penetration in terms of volume rather than value may be little higher than it then was. It had never risen above the 1979 level and the brunt of the deterioration in the industry's trading situation was borne by exports. Certainly by 1985 import penetration measured in current prices was a little lower than in 1979 and 1980, and the ratio of net exports to supplies was recovering fast.

The growth of import penetration in the late 1970s and the contraction of the trade surplus can be explained by the familiar rise in the ratio of export unit values to import unit values. In china and porcelain table-ware, it increased from 2.13 in 1977 to 2.98 in 1980 and then declined to 2.37 in 1985. In other tableware it rose from 1.23 to 1.88 and fell back to 1.38 in 1984; in 1985, however, it jumped to 1.69. The volume of exports fell by 40 per cent from the peak in 1977 to 1982. It has recovered since then but is still well short of what it was in the late

1970s. The fall was rather less in very high-quality porcelain and china, which also showed the biggest recovery; in 1984 and 1985, the volume of exports surpassed the late 1970s level. There was a correspondingly greater fall in other products where export volumes are still depressed. The volume of imports jumped by nearly three quarters between 1977 and 1979 but grew at a less hectic pace thereafter. Imports of porcelain and china and of ornamental ware, much of it of a kind not produced in this country, have continued to grow but the fall in imports of other table and kitchenware more than offset this rise, reflecting a cutback in purchases of cheap goods from Taiwan which were exceptionally large in 1980. Other low-cost suppliers, notably Portugal and South Korea, continue to gain ground but the import market as a whole is still dominated by the older Community countries and Japan.

Takeovers in the industry during the 1960s and 1970s resulted in the creation of two large firms, the Wedgwood Group and the Doulton Group, with turnover in the region of £150 million in both cases. Both are members of larger groups; Doulton has been owned by Pearsons since 1972, while Wedgwood was taken over by Waterford Glass in 1986. The next two largest producers have also been acquired by outsiders, Worcester by London International in 1984 and Staffordshire Potteries by Coloroll two years later. The size and strength of the leading firms has long been exceptional for a consumer goods industry, and has been reinforced by recent events. The four big producers account for perhaps three quarters of output by value; their precise share is uncertain because of the lack of information about sales by small producers which are thought to be rapidly increasing. The big producers, inheritors of a classical design tradition, lay great emphasis on their brand names, including those of firms taken over when the industry was consolidated. The Doulton group for example sells top-quality china and porcelain under the brand names Royal Doulton, Royal Crown Derby and Minton; Wedgwood uses its own name, Coalport, and Crown Staffordshire at the top of the market, selling lower-priced goods under other, less hallowed, names.

Retailing appears to be more diffuse than manufacturing. The Retail Enquiry provides little guidance because of the grouping of china with hardware and other items in most published data. In the group as a whole, a larger than average share of turnover, just over half in 1984, is in the hands of single-outlet and small multiple retailers. It is believed that small specialist china shops continue to have a large share of trade, even though the share of multiples and supermarkets is increasing at the lower end of the market where they sell pre-packaged own-brand goods. What principally distinguishes the retailing of domestic china from other consumer goods is the very active role taken by the manufacturers.

The bigger manufacturers run their own shops-within-shops; Doulton additionally owns the Lawley's chain of china and glass specialists; Wedgwood too owns a number of specialist outlets. The Price Commission and the Design Council both took the view that producers' retail interests had strengthened their position. Discussing the relatively low level of import penetration in this industry, the Mellor Report stated, 'It seems to us most likely that the UK market has been safeguarded by the fact that the indigenous product remains a remarkably good one, both in terms of quality and value, and that its built-in selling points have been assisted by the considerable control exerted ... by the UK manufacturers over the retail outlets'.[3]

The most important selling point of domestic tableware, however, is its appearance. Good design is critical. All large retailers consulted rated style and appearance very important. Quality and flexibility of supply ranked second, product performance and delivery third, followed by contact with suppliers; a majority of respondents rated them very important, the rest usually important. (These replies may have been influenced by the fact that no respondent was a china specialist, though several were, principally, retailers of household goods.) Novelty and promotion were generally no more than 'of some importance'. Small retailers dealing in china among other goods showed a similar pattern of preferences. Large retailers of china and earthenware were well satisfied with United Kingdom products and producers. They were clearly superior in all aspects of service to customers except delivery, and even here a majority found them as good or better. Save in novelty, they equalled or surpassed foreign competitors on design; but there were some criticisms of United Kingdom prices. This latter was confined to retailers serving the lower end of the market, who found the design of British products as good as or better than that of imports. At the top end, retailers were less enthusiastic about British design which was as good as but not better than that of overseas suppliers, but they were happy with prices. The proportion of imports was very low to average, with no noticeable difference among market sectors. Imports were purchased principally on grounds of price and non-availability, only occasionally because of design, and one respondent indicated that the limited production capacity of United Kingdom suppliers had led to an increase in imports. Lower prices for mass market goods might mean a reduction in imports, as would more adventurous design at the top end of the market. Comments by small china retailers, barring the somewhat prejudiced buyer referred to in Chapter 4, were similar though less enthusiastic. Like other small retailers, they were less happy than their large competitors about manufacturers' services, especially delivery. But by and large, retailers rated British goods and producers highly.

This industry has a less outstanding record than toiletries, possibly because its prices moved sharply out of line in the late 1970s and early 1980s, possibly also because it is more vulnerable to competition from the new industrial countries. The strengths of the industry lie in design and, judging by its greater success in containing import penetration than sustaining exports, in its exceptional position in respect of retailing. These strengths have enabled it to recoup its losses at home, even if it still has to recover fully its position in export markets.

WALLCOVERINGS

Official data on the wall coverings industry are even scantier than in the case of domestic china and earthenware. Neither an index of output nor of prices is available, and the quarterly enquiries on deliveries by the BSO cover a smaller proportion of employment in the industry, less than 85 per cent. The Wallcoverings Manufacturers Association (WMA) keeps its own records, but unfortunately for present purposes they ignore imports so that it is necessary to fall back on the official data.

Wallcoverings are made of a great variety of materials but the two most important by far are paper and vinyl. The Business Monitor distinguishes between finished wallpaper, which accounted for 27 per cent of the value of output in 1984, vinyls with 45 per cent of the value of output and other unspecified papers. In terms of volume, however, wallpaper is the more important with output exceeding 32 million rolls against vinyl's 31 million. Recorded deliveries of both types have fallen in recent years, but paperhangings have been the more seriously affected. Paper has also come under greater competition from imports which increased by almost half in terms of volume between 1979 and 1984 against less than a third for vinyl. In exports the position was reversed with vinyl sales falling more sharply than paper.

Domestic manufacturers have been successful in containing import penetration by keeping prices competitive, so that they have never lost their grip on the mass market, and by introducing a steady flow of products that are increasingly easy for the amateur to use. In papers especially imports are limited to specialist and high-quality products originating mainly in the rest of the Community. The ratio of domestic output unit values to import unit values has been less than unity since 1974. It rose rather sharply between 1980 and 1982, which certainly boosted the volume of imports from 1981 on. What has happened to relative prices since 1982 is not clear because of a change in definitions. Probably the ratio remains less favourable than it was in the late 1970s, and the rise in domestic prices may well have been a factor in depressing consumption. In vinyls, the ratio exceeds unity reflecting the superior quality of the domestic product. It rose very sharply in the late 1970s, from around 1.2 in 1974 to 1.4 in 1979 but began to fall in 1980 and by 1984 was back to 1.2. Since 1980, the unit value of domestic output has risen remarkably slowly, by 12.5 per cent in all, serving both to maintain consumption rather more than in the case of paper and to check the growth of imports. The unit value of exports, by contrast, continued to rise after 1980 and the volume of exports was halved.

The three largest producers, Coloroll, Crown and Weston-Hyde (formerly ICI but now only 50 per cent ICI-owned), probably have between them something like 60 per cent of the market in terms of volume, while there are several other sizeable firms and a fringe of small producers, some of them design-led. Within the past few years, American and Swiss firms have bought up some of the large producers, including Crown, but this has not yet affected the industry's performance. All the major manufacturers have their own well-known brands and do their own designing, although they have been somewhat neglectful of both marketing and styling. Product development has been directed towards producing new kinds of paper – ready-pasted, blown goods, strippable and peelable paper – rather than up-grading the appearance and presentation of their products. Coloroll is the exception. The rise in its share of the market, reportedly from 3 to 30 per cent within eight years, is the result of aggressive marketing and of skilful promotion of coordinates.

The large producers sell to large retailers. The 1984 Retail Enquiry showed almost 90 per cent of wallcoverings being sold by retailers of household goods, principally of course the big DIY chains. There is an interesting contrast between the retailing of paint and wallcoverings. There is tremendous pressure to treat paint as a commodity, and in consequence a rapid advance in the sale of own brands. In wallcoverings the design initiative remains with the manufacturers and their brands. The buying power of their retail customers still poses problems for manufacturers but the disparity between buyers and sellers appears to be less here than in many other consumer goods industries while the large share of exports in production, still equivalent to almost one third of the value of total deliveries, gives them a wider and possibly more profitable market.

The only retailers consulted about wall coverings were the big DIY groups. They proved on the whole to be equally concerned about the price of the product and elements of design, as also about delivery. All were rated very important in most cases though there were differences of emphasis between respondents. There was no clear pattern discernible in relation to other buying factors among the small numbers of replies received. This was the one industry where there was difficulty in obtaining information from retailers because imports of several firms consulted

were nil or negligible and they did not therefore complete the questionnaires. Even those that did reply were not heavily dependent on imports,
which accounted for more than 10 per cent of purchases in only one
instance. Imports were most commonly purchased directly or via manufacturers. Respondents generally considered British products and producers as good as or better than their foreign competitors in all respects
and it may safely be assumed that those who did not import shared
their opinion. There were some mild criticisms of design among retailers
and prices of some British goods were higher than those of imports.
Greater attention to style and appearance was mentioned as the change
most likely to lead to larger purchases of British goods. For the present,
however, the only reason given for importing was that comparable goods
were not available in the United Kingdom.

  To sum up, toiletries, domestic china, and wallcoverings have certain
features in common that help to explain the more than average successful
performance of these industries in resisting import penetration. The most
obvious is that, although their prices did move out of line with those
of their competitors in the late 1970s, except perhaps in toiletries, they
have on the evidence of retail buyers been brought back into line, or
very nearly so. Second, manufacturers' brands predominate in all three;
their products have retained their identity for the final consumer. This
advantage has not been exploited as well as it might except by the major
manufacturers of domestic china; yet the impression remains that producers are more in control of their selling and more active sellers than
in many other industries. New products and designs have been developed
by the producers themselves, though in domestic china and perhaps
in wallcoverings there is a feeling that still more could be done. Finally
in all three there are larger firms that can cope with the large retailers,
even though they may complain of their practices. Thus the relatively
successful performance of these industries is due not to any one factor
but to a mixture of strengths that was not found in the other industries
examined.

10

CONCLUSION

THE GROWTH OF IMPORT PENETRATION

It was pointed out in Chapter 2 that, between 1974 and 1984, the volume of manufactured consumer goods imported into the United Kingdom more than doubled, and import penetration, measured as the ratio of the value of imports to apparent consumption, rose by 17 percentage points from 19 per cent to 36 per cent. On average, import penetration rose rather faster from 1979 to 1984 than from 1974 to 1979 because of the surge in imports from 1979 to 1982 associated with the rise in the exchange rate and the loss of price competitiveness in the late 1970s. There was, however, great variety of experience among individual industries, as the case studies show. Import penetration rose rather less rapidly after 1979 than before in clothing and knitwear, in cosmetics and toiletries, and in domestic china, as also in some industries not covered by the case studies, notably consumer electronics. Since 1982, the rate of growth of import penetration has slackened although some of the industries examined are again exceptions to the general pattern. Generally speaking, however, import penetration in recent years has been growing at a rate close to and occasionally below that obtaining in the latter half of the 1970s. The one notable exception to this rule that was identified in the case studies was domestic electric appliances. In other instances of more rapid growth, such as toiletries, special factors appear to have been operating.

The slackening in the rate of growth of import penetration has been accompanied by a recovery in output from the 1982 low but in 1985 production of consumer goods was generally lower than in the late 1970s. Again the case studies provided examples of exceptions to this pattern: non-knit clothing, domestic electric appliances, toiletries and probably china. Among other consumer goods industries for which production indices are available, only consumer electronics has surpassed the 1979 level of output. These exceptions illustrate the overriding importance of the growth of domestic demand rather than import penetration on output. All have faced relatively buoyant demand, but some – domestic electric appliances and toiletries – have at the same time had high or rising rates of import penetration. Conversely, in several of the traditional household goods industries where the growth of import penetration has decelerated, production has recovered much less because demand remains slack. In short, rising import penetration is neither the only or necessarily the most important reason for the contraction of output in British consumer goods industries.

One of the principal objects of this study was to discover by means of questionnaires and interviews why retailers purchase imports rather than domestic products for resale. The reason most often quoted was that comparable goods are not available in the United Kingdom. As shown in Chapter 4, it was mentioned in almost 40 per cent of replies to questionnaires and frequently aired in interviews. This is not to imply a shortage of products in the United Kingdom but rather the increasing search for variety to stimulate and satisfy the consumer. Price was almost as important, mentioned in about one third of replies, but design and quality rather less, mentioned in about one in five of replies. Other reasons were mentioned, but they were of comparatively little significance. It was clear from replies to questionnaires, and this point was reinforced many times in interviews, that the decision to import often has more than one motive. Almost half the replies to questionnaires mentioned two out of the three, non-availability, price and design, or all three together. If a single reason was given, it was most likely to be that comparable goods are not available, or, though this was less common, that foreign products are cheaper. Design was seldom the sole reason for importing. Retailers are looking for value for money, an appropriate combination of price and design features, and though they may be prepared to pay more for excellence in design, they will not move far outside their normal price range.

There are, of course, differences of emphasis as the case studies showed. Price emerged as the prime reason for importing men's suits, and was also of more than average importance in toiletries, china and earthenware and household textiles. A number of replies to questionnaires relating to carpets and domestic metalware (saucepans and the like) suggested that it is also the principal motive for imports in these sectors. The lack of comparable British goods was more important for clothing in general, for domestic electrical products and, it may safely be assumed, for electronic consumer goods, for certain items in the cosmetic and toiletries group and also, again judging only by replies to questionnaires, for footwear. Design, in particular style and appearance, strongly influenced imports of clothing and domestic electric appliances. It was much less important in relation to other products, though in the case of almost every product covered by the questionnaires it was mentioned by some respondents as a reason for importing. Cosmetics and toiletries and wallcoverings were the only certain exception. It was not mentioned in connection with carpets, but the number of respondents in this case was very small. On the other hand, British carpets have a good reputation for design.

The fact that so much emphasis is laid by retailers on importing goods otherwise unavailable in order to widen the range on offer and satisfy the consumer's desire for variety is sufficient explanation of the uninterrupted growth of import penetration over the past decade. Given that British accession to the European Community made it easier to import as well as, to some extent, reducing import prices by abolishing or reducing tariffs, this motive was probably of overwhelming importance from 1974 to 1978 or thereabouts, since relative prices were then moving in Britain's favour. It was strongly reinforced when the price of British goods moved out of line with competing products in the late 1970s. The effects of the rise in prices on exports and the balance of trade was devastating, but there is no evidence to support the view that import penetration would not have continued to rise had relative prices remained unchanged. It would merely have increased less rapidly.

It was said in Chapter 2 that the continuation of very rapid growth in import penetration in recent years was somewhat puzzling, given the fall in the price of British goods relative to imports shown by comparing domestic producer prices and import unit values. The case studies suggest that in fact British goods are not competitive on price even now, that the relative price index gave a false reading. Where it was possible to devise some measure of relative prices for specific products that permitted comparison between 1977 or thereabouts, when British prices were competitive, and the mid-1980s, it emerged that although British prices are lower in relation to those of their competitors than they were around 1980 and 1981, they were by 1985 still not back to where they were in 1977, and that there was a disquieting tendency for relative British prices to start rising again. Replies to questionnaires and interviews, which reflect the situation in 1986, told the same story: British goods were not yet fully competitive on price, though with the fall in the exchange rate things were moving in the right direction. Again there is considerable variation between sectors. The three 'successful' industries, toiletries, china and wallcoverings, were judged to have prices equal to or lower than those of their competitors, as did the domestic electric appliances industry; but in every other instance British prices were higher. Outside the four industries mentioned above, very few respondents judged British prices to be lower than those of comparable imports and many more, in some cases such as knitwear, household textiles and hardware, a majority of all respondents found British goods more expensive. This is the more worrying since prices in consumer goods industries, both individually and collectively, have risen less than United Kingdom producer prices in general since 1979.

Inability to compete on prices is not confined to goods coming from the Far East and other low-cost suppliers. In certain lines they have an unassailable price advantage, as witness the unit values quoted in the case studies. The gap between British and West European prices is narrower than that between Britain and the low-cost producers but it is still there in Britain's disfavour. It is not a question of importing on grounds of price from say the Far East and of design and lack of comparable British goods from France, Italy or Germany. The only distinction that retailers were prepared to make in discussion was between the goods themselves. A particular item might be cheaper in one country, another elsewhere. The questionnaire replies support this approach. There was no significant difference in the origin of imports purchased by retailers solely because they were cheaper or because of non-price factors alone. Both groups purchased equally from Western Europe, Eastern Europe, the Far East and elsewhere.

Price performance has improved but not enough, and the same is true of design, though the record here is better. There are several industries where the style and appearance, the quality and the performance of British goods are on average judged to be as good as or better than foreign products. This is true of wallcoverings, china, household textiles, carpets, metalware, furniture and, with some reservations about quality, cosmetics and toiletries. Clothing, footwear and electrical appliances came down very badly on style and appearance and clothing was, with exceptions, severely criticised for poor quality. No industry came out well on novelty or technological innovation. The other general weakness was that, where the market is segmented by class and income, design was found wanting at the higher end even though it was satisfactory in the mass market. This point emerged both from the broad analysis of Chapter 4 and in the case studies. Even where retailers took a generally favourable view of the design of British goods, as in household textiles, those at the top of the market were inclined to be critical.

A major weakness found in many industries was performance on delivery. British producers were slower and in particular less reliable than their competitors. The division here was not so much between industries as between customers. The larger retailers were well served by their suppliers; the independents were not. With regard to other elements of service to customers – promotion, contact between customer and suppliers, suppliers' knowledge of the market and flexibility – the larger retailers were again better, in fact very well served. Save in a few instances, however, it is unlikely that import penetration was much affected by difficulties in dealing with British rather than foreign suppliers, despite the criticisms voiced by small retailers.

THE EFFECT OF LARGE-SCALE RETAILING ON IMPORTS

As noted in Chapter 3, it is widely believed that the large scale of retailing in the United Kingdom has promoted imports; and judging from replies to questionnaires, large British retailers are indeed heavily engaged in direct importing. There are theoretical reasons for believing that firms with substantial purchasing power will be more import-dependent than small firms, though it should be noted that this applies equally to retailers and wholesalers. It is the size of units in distribution rather than in retailing that matters. However, the contention that large-scale retailing in the United Kingdom has raised the level of import penetration cannot be proved or disproved, but little evidence was found to suggest that it had, while there is a good deal to suggest that its influence has been greatly exaggerated.

In one or two instances, large retailers commented that because output by individual British producers was small they were constrained to purchase overseas, or that they imported partly in order to avoid excessive dependence on a small number of British suppliers. This could be interpreted as large-scale retailing fostering imports; equally, it could be said that the small size or number of British manufacturers promoted imports. The case studies showed widely different patterns between industries. In clothing and in household textiles, it appeared that large retailers may be the principal importers; in domestic electric appliances probably and in furniture certainly, manufacturers import more than retailers. Evidence on the other industries studied was scantier, but at least in cosmetics and toiletries intra-manufacturer importing is thought to be substantial. Nor does it appear that the degree of import penetration bears any close relation to the purchasing channels involved.

As was said earlier, the country's largest retailer relies very little on imports. Marks and Spencer has deliberately fostered domestic production of goods that were initially imported and sold well as it has branched out into new lines. Other big retailers pursue a similar policy, if less publicly and less successfully. Retailers are well aware that their business depends on consumers' incomes and that a substantial slice of income still originates in British industry. It is not only the Electricity Boards that prefer to buy British in order to stimulate demand, even if other retailers are less able to do so directly.

It was possible to make a rough check on whether very large-scale retailing was associated with higher import dependence than retailing by multiples in general. Looking at the share of imports in purchases by the top twenty and in purchases by other retailers, apart from the independents, there was no discernible difference on account of size. It may be that the sample was biased. Not all firms in the top twenty were prepared to cooperate with our enquiries and the suspicion remains that this was partly because they were very heavy importers. There clearly are instances where the development of own-branding by retailers could have raised the level of imports, but in the one instance where it is known that own brands are almost entirely imported, that is in domestic electric appliances, the manufacturers themselves have resorted to large-scale importing. However, the relationship between retailers' own brands and imports would bear further examination.

From the research described here, it appears that the level of imports by retailers is determined first by the goods concerned and secondly by policy at the level of the individual company. The average level of import dependence by respondents to the questionnaires accords fairly well with the import penetration ratio for the product group in question, being for example high in knitwear and footwear, and low in wall coverings and toiletries. The correspondence is not perfect but it is good enough. At the same time, within most product groups every degree of import dependence from very low to very high can be found. Where a retailer replied to questionnaires on several products, import dependence varied widely from product to product. And although the independents were not asked directly about the share of imports in sales, the origin of their supplies, the extensive contacts with foreign manufacturers and importers that they reported, suggests that their dependence on imports is as high as that of the large retailers. It is unnecessary to invoke the scale of retailing to explain the level of import penetration, for it is readily explicable by other factors.

RELATIONS BETWEEN RETAILERS AND MANUFACTURERS

While large retailers may be acquitted of the charge of raising the level of import penetration, they may nevertheless have aggravated the problems faced by British consumer goods industries. It was shown in the case studies that the purchasing power of the largest retailers was as large as and in some cases very much larger than the turnover of the biggest manufacturers. Where similar calculations can be made for other industries, in for example footwear and carpets, the same situation obtains, although the ratios are never so large as in clothing and knitwear and in furniture. The existence of market power, at least among the biggest retailers, is widespread. The ratios on which this assertion is based referred to 1984. In the past two years, the market power of some retailers, particularly of specialist retailers, has been vastly increased by takeovers and mergers. Organic growth among the larger firms in coming years is likely to raise it still further.

The Office of Fair Trading has adopted the attitude that retailing is a highly competitive business, which is true, and claims that the price reductions secured from manufacturers have been passed on to the consumer, again probably true; though it should be noted that its evidence comes almost exclusively from the food industries and the grocery trade and may not be applicable to non-food retailing. The possible longer-run consequences for British industry of increasing retail market power – lower profitability and insecurity – seem to have been ignored. They were discussed by the Monopolies and Mergers Commission[1] in their report on Discounts to Retailers; but at least so far as discounts were concerned, the Commission judged 'that the ... practice, where it has been a feature of enhanced competition among manufacturers, has tended to improve efficiency and induce economies'. Since concentration in retailing as measured by the BSO remains fairly low, the problem has been pushed under the carpet. We are now approaching the point where concentration itself could become a serious problem in certain sectors and may begin to restrict consumer choice. At the very least then, mergers or takeovers among the biggest retailers should be closely scrutinised and if possible prevented.

Producers of consumer goods, accustomed to a sellers' market, let the initiative pass to the retailers. In particular, many manufacturers are now in a position where they have lost any control of the price at which they can sell their goods, not because they are operating in the economist's perfect market but because they are facing dominant buyers. In the clothing and related industries the leading producers are attempting to resolve this problem by matching size with size, undertaking their own mergers, but that is hardly feasible in many consumer goods industries nor in our view is it desirable. The excessive centralisation that went with the creation of large firms in the 1970s benefited no-one, least of all the firms concerned. There are acceptable alternatives: to work very closely with carefully chosen retailers and grow as they grow, as Marks and Spencer's suppliers have done; to specialise and develop a strong identity, which may require some direct involvement in retailing though this has its disadvantages as well as advantages. For the smaller manufacturer, there is the choice of cooperating with small retailers, to the benefit of both and of the public which may thereby be supplied with a greater variety of goods, of cooperating with other small producers to secure some of the financial and marketing advantages of size, or again of specialising, finding their own niche in the market as many new small firms are doing. What is required in every case is an active marketing policy. Manufacturers could well copy the approach of successful retailers and study not only how to satisfy a particular set of customers but also how to create or promote demand for their products.

There is, as the retailers themselves pointed out, a variety of successful firms in all industries, but where a whole industry has performed well in the face of increasing competition from imports, one element has been that the leading producers are sufficiently strong to deal on something like equal terms with the large retailers. But this, of course, is only one strand in the pattern of success. In the more successful industries, manufacturers had got everything right – price, design and service to customers; or at least a sufficiently large part of the industry had done so to check the growth of import penetration and sustain a reasonable export trade.

DEFINITIONS AND SOURCES

The data on import penetration and net export ratios in table 2.4 were derived by summing the grossed up value of output of the relevant industries and trade figures reclassified according to the SIC. Original figures for output were obtained from the Quarterly Business Monitors, the Business Statistics Office, and the Department of Trade and Industry. Trade figures were obtained from MQ10 'Overseas trade analysed in terms of industries', and its predecessor M10. The coverage of the various groups is shown in the table at the end of this appendix, which also lists the SITC headings used to calculate the data in table 2.6. It should be noted that the coverage of SIC 1968 is rather wider than that of the SIC 1980 headings used, while the SITC figures do not cover all the trade of the industries concerned.

Data in chapters 5 to 9 inclusive are derived from the following sources, unless otherwise indicated:

Demand: Consumers' expenditure: *United Kingdom National Accounts 1986 Edition*. The figures in source are derived from the Retail Enquiries, adjusted to include expenditure in N. Ireland, etc., and are therefore consistent in coverage with the Retail Enquiry data used to indicate market size. The expenditure figures generally cover part of the output of other industries besides those being examined. For example, expenditure on clothing includes some outlays on other textile products as well as knitwear and clothing.

Output value: Quarterly Business Monitors. Figures refer to estimates of sales of the relevant products, grossed up to allow for sales by small firms. In many cases firms covered by the quarterly enquiries account for only 70 per cent or less of the industry's sales, so the grossing up factor is very large.

Output volume: Quarterly Business Monitors. The output indices are intended to measure changes in the volume of industrial activity of establishments classified to the industry, including their output of other goods but excluding the output of the industry's characteristic products by firms classified to other industries. In some cases, an indicator of the volume of all deliveries of the relevant products is published in *British Business* which provides a superior measure of the volume of goods available from domestic production. Where the two series can be compared, they usually move fairly closely together in the long run, though they may diverge from year to year.

Import penetration and net trade ratios: Business Monitor M12 and MQ12. Additional estimates were derived from grossed up output and trade data classified by industry.

Volume and value of trade: Overseas Trade Statistics of the United Kingdom.

Table A1.1. *Coverage of tables 2.4 to 2.6*

SIC 1968	SIC 1980	Description in SIC 1980	Approximate SITC equivalent SITC R	SITC R2
Clothing and footwear				
417.1	4363	Hosiery & other weft-knitted goods and fabrics	Included with clothing	
450	451	Footwear	851	851
441–9	453	Clothing, hats and gloves	841	84
Electrical and electronic goods				
399(9)	3165	Domestic heating & cooking appliances	697.1	697.3
365(2)	3454	Electronic consumer goods & other electronic equipment n.e.s.	724.1/2 & 891.11	761/2 & 763.81, .88
368	346	Domestic-type electric appliances	725	775
Other household goods				
ex 463	2479.1	Domestic and ornamental glassware	665.2	665.2
ex 462	2489.3	Domestic china and other pottery	666	666
392	3162	Cutlery, spoons, forks, etc., razors & razor blades	696	696
399(6)	3167	Domestic and similar utensils of metal	697.2, .91	697.4, .81
419	438	Carpets, carpeting and rugs	657	659 less .3, .7 & 893.91/2
ex 473	4555	Soft furnishings	656.91	658.4
422(1)	4557	Household textiles		
472	4671	Wooden and upholstered furniture	821.01, .03, .09	821.11, .22, .92, .99
484(1)	4721	Wall coverings	641.97	641.97
492	4833	Plastic floor coverings	Included with carpets	
Other goods				
ex 275	ex 2581	Soap	554.1	554.1
273	2582	Perfumes, cosmetics & toilet preparations	553	553
432	442	Leather goods	831	831
494(1–2)	4941	Toys and games	894.2	894.2
494(3)	4942	Sports goods	894.4	894.71/2

Prices and unit values: Producer price indices published in *British Business* and in the *Quarterly Business Monitors*. Unit values were derived from output and trade data in the *Business Monitors* and from the *Overseas Trade Statistics*.

Manufacturing – number of enterprises, employment and concentration: Census of Production 1979–1983. Figures for years before 1979, classified according to SIC 1968, can rarely be reconciled with those for 1979 onwards, classified according to SIC 1980. In the 1984 Census, a new register of businesses was used so that the results are not comparable with those of previous years. It seemed best to ignore it in considering the changes from 1979 to 1983 resulting from the recession. The 1984 Census was used to calculate the ratio of manufacturers' sales to retailers' purchases.

Retailing – shares of independents and multiples, specialisation and concentration: Retail Enquiries. Data on product sales appear to be reasonably consistent between the different years, though the figures may have been affected by changes in the method of estimating sales by small retailers. Unfortunately it is impossible to check whether this is in fact so. It seems likely that, if anything, the share of small retailers in earlier years may be understated.

TURNOVER OF MAJOR NON-FOOD RETAILERS
1976–84

Data on retail turnover in the accompanying table have been collected primarily from company reports. In principle the figures refer to retail turnover in the United Kingdom exclusive of VAT. In some cases, however, some turnover from non-retail activities or from retailing outside the United Kingdom may be included, as indicated in footnotes to the table. The amounts involved are generally small. Turnover from leased departments is included, which may have led to some double counting, though the only significant instance appears to be the overlap between Harris Queensway and Debenhams in 1984 calendar equivalent. Turnover from businesses subsequently disposed of is generally included but there are some exceptions (see below).

Accounts referring to financial years ending in the months January to June inclusive are taken as equivalent to the preceding calendar year; for example, the twelve months ending in March 1985 are taken as equivalent to calendar 1984. Financial years ending in July to December are taken as equivalent to the calendar year in which the accounting year ends; thus the twelve months ending in August 1984 are taken as equivalent to calendar 1984. Where accounts relate to periods of more or less than 52 weeks they have been adjusted *pro rata*. Where turnover figures are not available for one of the years for which firms are ranked by turnover (1976, 1980 and 1984) as is the case with some firms that have recently been taken over, they are ranked by turnover in the preceding year.

Particularly in the early years of the period, a number of firms reported turnover inclusive of VAT. In such cases, turnover exclusive of VAT has been estimated by reference to the incidence of VAT on firms with a similar pattern of retailing and to the Retail Enquiries. Estimates of retail turnover have also been derived from incomplete information in company reports. Most of these estimates are reasonably firmly based but there are some firms notoriously chary of supplying information about their activities, notably C. & A. Modes, for which the figures shown in the table are at best informed guesses and probably on the conservative side. It is believed that the ranking of retailers by turnover is not seriously affected by the inclusion of such estimates.

One group of retailers has, of necessity, been entirely omitted from the table: the retail organisations that are part of major manufacturing enterprises for which no separate data on turnover are available. Among them are the retail outlets operated by Coats Patons, Courtaulds, C. & J. Clark, Wedgwood and Royal Doulton, and Thorn-EMI (the Rumbelows chain). Some of these would certainly qualify for inclusion among the top fifty retailers in the United Kingdom. Similarly, certain retailers with substantial manufacturing activities (Laura Ashley, Raybeck, Magnet and Southerns) have been omitted because it proved impossible to make reasonable estimates of their retail turnover. Halfords has been omitted since, although it is a major High Street retailer, its business in car and cycle parts falls outside the scope of this survey.

It has to be admitted that the selection of firms at the tail of the distribution may be somewhat inaccurate – some that should be included are omitted and vice versa[1] – because of the difficulty of getting reliable and consistent data. Thus the ranking of the tail-enders may be incorrect; but it is unlikely that this seriously affects the estimated total turnover of the top fifty retailers.

All firms that are believed to have figured in the top fifty in 1976, 1980 or 1984 are included in the table with the exception of Hardy and Co which ranked 30 in 1976, Henderson Kenton (44) and Maples (42). The first two were taken over by Harris Queensway before 1980, the third by Waring and Gillow. (Two other firms that only ranked in 1976 are also omitted from the table.) There has been a considerable amount of takeover activity during the period, mostly of smaller chains or individual stores by members of the top fifty, and more recently there have been several major takeovers or mergers between members of the top fifty. Some of these show up in the table; those that have occurred subsequent to 1984 are discussed in Chapter 3. It may be useful to add some comment on the chequered history of one or two groups here.

Allied Retailers was taken over by ADG in 1978, when it also acquired Wades. The figures for 1979 to 1981 refer to the turnover of ADG's 'furniture and carpet group', those for 1982 and 1983 to the turnover reported for Allied Carpets and Wades. The latter was sold during the course of 1984 and 1984 turnover relates to Allied Carpets only. The *Burton Group's* turnover from the Ryman chain, sold in 1981, has been excluded throughout. The reported turnover of *Dixons* and *Woolworths* in 1984 included sales by Curry's and Comet respectively for part of the year only; figures in the table have been adjusted to indicate the approximate combined turnover for the whole of the financial year equivalent to 1984. Woolworths' 1982 turnover is a 'notional' figure, calculated in source on the basis of what it would have been had Woolworths Holdings been in existence for twelve months. Likewise the *Habitat/Mothercare* figures for 1981 are the group's own estimate of what their combined turnover would have been had they merged at the beginning of the financial year 1981/2. The 1982 figure for *UDS* is a forecast for the turnover of continuing businesses, following the sale of the John Collier and Richards chains. Turnover in 1984, after the takeover by Hanson Trust, relates to Allders Department Stores and Ocean Trading (duty-free shops) only, the remaining business having been disposed of.

Table A2.1. The top fifty United Kingdom retailers

Turnover in £ million

Calendar year equivalent	Major retail activities	1976	Ranking	1977	1978	1979	1980	Ranking	1981	1982	1983	1984	Ranking	Financial year ending in
Allied Retailers/ADG[a]	C	53	23	66	(70)[b]	125[c]	128[c]	25	118[c]	113	120|	82	35	Apr
Argos (BAT) Industries PLC	F	26	39	49	85	129[x]	140	23	167	207	247	311	20	Nov/Dec
Austin Reed Group PLC[d]	A_1	18	45	20	22	24	23[x]	50	26	28	32	34	50	Jan
Bentalls PLC	F	32	36	36	42	45	45	41	48	54	58	61	41	Jan
British Home Stores PLC[e]	F	232	10	260	307	366	410	10	428	456	494	550	12	Mar
Boots Co. PLC	F	628	4	743	859	981	1135	2	1237	1351	1457	1565	3	Mar
British Gas Corporation (appliance trading only)	D	120	18	145	184	199	204	17	212	215	219	237	22	Mar
Burton Group PLC[d]	A_1	100[c]	19	110[c]	112[c]	112	149	21	170	200	258	360	16	Aug
C. & A. Modes Ltd	A_1	(160)	13	...	...	...	(260)	13	...	...	...	(350)	17	...
Combined English Stores Group PLC	E	43[b]	29	44[b]	55[b]	69	78	31	69	68	74	82	36	Jan
Comet	B	47	26	83	124	164	192	19	196	239	317	T/O	–	Aug
Courts (Furnishers) PLC[c]	C	26[d]	40	30[d]	34[d]	36	37	44	38	40	44	48	46	Mar
Currys Group PLC	B	129[d]	17	146[d]	171[d]	195	228	16	243	294	343	T/O	–	Jan
Debenhams PLC	F	302[d]	8	348[d]	406[d]	424[d]	494[d]	8	542[d]	554[d]	610[b]	644[b]	10	Jan
Dixons Group PLC	BE			53	69	87	103	28	117	151	217|	671[x]	8	Apr
The Electricity Council (appliance trading only)	B	142	14	154	196	240	252	14	267	307	351	388	14	Mar
Empire Stores (Bradford) PLC[e]	G	77	20	93	109	133	143	22	139	142	154	157	25	Jan
Etam PLC	A_1	...	...	...	...	15	22	...	28	36	48	56	44	Jan
Fenwicks Ltd	F	32	35	40	50	58	66	34	68	73	81	90	33	Jan
Fine Art Developments PLC[b]	G	(20)	43	(27)[d]	(33)[d]	(43)[d]	(48)[d]	39	(48)[d]	(49)[d]	(65)[d]	(100)	30	Mar
Foster Bros Clothing PLC	A_1	41[d]	31	47[d]	63[d]	82[d]	84[d]	30	81	74	91	...	32	Feb

Freemans PLC	G	131	16	155	186	209	229	15	257	279	282	318	19	Jan
George Oliver (Footwear) PLC	B_2	..	..	..	..	..	..	..	18	32	37	39	49	Dec
A. Goldberg & Sons PLC	F	17	48	21	25[x]	29	30	47	33	33	34	33	..	Feb/Mar
Grattan PLC	G	138[d]	15	155	176	215	200	18	177	183	195	219	23	Jan
Great Universal Stores PLC	ACDG	636[d]	2	737[d]	873[d]	1057[d]	1037[d]	3	1045[d]	1122	1248	1336	4	Mar
Habitat/Habitat Mothercare	CD/A_1CD	..	..	20[b]	26[b]	33[b]	37	43|	179	211	259	301[x]	21	Jun/Mar
Harris Queensway PLC	C	15	49	30	53	80	117	26	138	172	225	370	15	Dec
Homebase (Sainsbury PLC)	D	..	..	..	..	..	..	..	..	..	40[b]	64	40	Mar
Home Charm Group PLC[ce]	D	17	46	22	29	41	60	36	74	106	137	183	24	Dec
House of Fraser PLC	F	401[b]	7	466[b]	542[b]	604[b]	665[b]	7	706	744	815	898	7	Jan
James Beattie PLC	F	23	41	26	30	33	34	45	33	35	38	42	48	Jan
John Lewis Partnership PLC[a]	F	203[b]	11	238[b]	290[b]	332[b]	370[d]	11	386[d]	436[d]	502[d]	561[d]	11	Jan
Lasky's (Ladbroke Group PLC)	B	..	..	..	3	11	24	49	28	46	66	67[d]	39	Dec/Jan
Littlewoods Organisation PLC	G	564	5	656	784	904	956	4	945	1038	1042	1023	6	Dec
Mackays Stores (Holdings) Ltd[c]	A_1	..	..	..	..	..	30[b]	46	31	36	36	36	..	Apr
MFI Furniture Group PLC	C	34	34	56	88	127	191	20	176	246	301	328[x]	18	May
Marks & Spencer PLC	F	1065	1	1254	1473	1668	1873	1	2199	2506	2855	3194	1	Mar
Mothercare	A_1/	70	21	89	106	130	136	24	T/O	..	..	..	..	Feb/Mar
John Menzies PLC[b]	F	(65)	22	(76)	(89)	(99)	(110)	27	(118)	(121)	(139)	(152)	26	Jan/Feb
Next PLC (formerly J. Hepworth & Sons PLC)	A_1	28[b]	38	34[b]	41[b]	50[b]	60	35	74	82	97	106	29	Aug
Owen Owen PLC	F	50[d]	24	54[d]	64[d]	69[d]	74[d]	32	77	78	84	89	34	Jan
Payless (Marley PLC)	D	..	..	..	..	..	..	..	35	52[x]	75	91	31	Oct/Dec
H Samuel Group	E	46	27	54	65	73	69	33	68	68	79	108	28	Jan
Sears PLC[a]	A_2EF	416	6	450	573	656	733	6	842	940	1108	1239	5	Jan
W H Smith & Sons (Holdings) PLC[d]	DF	165	12	202	250	313	368	12	415	469	522[x]	667	9	Jan/Jun
A. G. Stanley Holdings PLC	D	12	..	16	22	38	50[c]	38	52[c]	51	52	53	45	Dec
Stylo PLC[c]	A_2F	17	47	20	24	..	28	48	39	47	49	59	42	Jan

Table A2.1. (*contd.*)

Calendar year equivalent	Major retail activities	1976	Rank-ing	1977	1978	1979	1980	Rank-ing	1981	1982	1983	1984	Rank-ing	Financial year ending in
Superdrug	E	...	...	20	27	37	51	37	63	81	102	129^x	27	Feb
Telefusion PLC^e	B	40	32	38	50	47	44	42	52^b	61^b	65^b	59^b	43	Apr
UDS/Allders (Hanson Trust PLC)	F	296	9	331	395	445	449	9	436	379|	...	389|	13	Jan/Sept
Ward White Group PLC	A$_2$	...	...	...	...	...	...	...	...	8^x	41	74	38	Jan
Waring & Gillow (Holdings) PLC	C	40	33	45	58	63^c	88^b	29	80^b	78	78	...	37	Mar
Henry Wigfall & Son PLC^c	B	31	37	34	...	44	45	40	42	41	41	46	47	Mar
F. W. Woolworth PLC/ Woolworth Holdings PLC	F/DF/BDF	634	3	702	799	862|	925	5	1015|	1101	1251	|1776^x	2	Jan

^{a} Excludes turnover from food retailing.
^{b} Estimates from incomplete data; figures in brackets are very rough estimates.
^{c} May include some non-retail turnover.
^{d} Estimated from turnover including VAT.
^{e} May include some overseas turnover.

Notes: Column 2: Major retail activities relate to; A$_1$ Clothing; A$_2$ Footwear; B Electronic and electrical goods; C Furniture, carpets and household textiles; D DIY, hardware, china and glass, and gas appliances; E Other specialist retailing; F Mixed retail business; G Mail order. The classification of retail activities is based on that used in the Retail Enquiries. Retailers dealing principally in food, drink and confectionery, tobacco and newspapers are excluded, as are retailers of motor car parts and related products, and hire and repair.
\| indicates a discontinuity in series because of change in accounting year, major takeover or merger.
x = figures adjusted to 52-week period.
... = not in top 50.
T/O = taken over or merged.

QUESTIONNAIRES SENT TO LARGE AND SMALL RETAILERS

LARGE RETAILERS

Confidential

IMPORT PENETRATION AND DISTRIBUTION: [PRODUCT DESCRIPTION]

The following questions relate to research being undertaken by the National Institute of Economic and Social Research into the reasons for purchasing imports rather than UK-manufactured goods.

1. Please indicate how you assess the following factors in making purchasing decisions by placing a tick in the appropriate column:

	Very important	Important	Some importance	Does not matter
1. Price				
2. Style and appearance				
3. Quality of materials and workmanship				
4. Product performance				
5. Novelty/technological innovation				
6. Speed and reliability of delivery				
7. Advertising and promotion by supplier				
8. Close and frequent contact with supplier				
9. Supplier's knowledge of market				
10. Flexibility of supply				

If you consider any other factor important, please specify.

2. In respect of these same factors, how would you rate British as compared to foreign products and producers? Please tick the appropriate column:

British are:	Better	About the same	Worse
1. Price*			
2. Style and appearance			
3. Quality of materials and workmanship			
4. Product performance			
5. Novely/technological performance			
6. Speed and reliability of delivery			
7. Advertising and promotion by supplier			
8. Close and frequent contact with supplier			
9. Supplier's knowledge of market			
10. Flexibility of supply			

* Better – lower British price.

3. What is the approximate share of imported goods in your purchases for resale? Please tick the appropriate box.

Less than 10 per cent	[ ]
10 to 25 per cent	[ ]
Over 25 to 40 per cent	[ ]
Over 40 per cent	[ ]
Don't know	[ ]

4. What are your reasons for purchasing imported rather than British goods? Please tick the appropriate box or boxes.

Imported goods are cheaper	[ ]
Imported products are better in design and quality	[ ]
Foreign suppliers (and importers) are easier to deal with than British producers	[ ]
Comparable goods are not made in the UK	[ ]
Other reasons (please specify)	

5. By what channels do you obtain imported goods? Please tick the appropriate box or boxes.

Direct purchase abroad and via import agents and/or associated companies	[ ]
Import merchants	[ ]
Wholesalers	[ ]
UK manufacturer-importers	[ ]
Other	[ ]

6. If you purchase abroad directly, in what areas do you buy? Please tick the appropriate box or boxes.

W. Europe	[ ]	Other Far East and Asia	[ ]
E. Europe including USSR	[ ]	Latin America	[ ]
USA	[ ]	Africa	[ ]
Japan	[ ]	Other	[ ]

7. To what market sectors are you selling? Please tick the appropriate boxes.

Age groups		*Social class*	
Under 25 years	[ ]	A and B	[ ]
25 to 40 years	[ ]	C	[ ]
Over 40	[ ]	D and E	[ ]
All	[ ]	All	[ ]

SMALL RETAILERS

For Retailers only: CONFIDENTIAL

IMPORT PENETRATION AND DISTRIBUTION

The following questions relate to research being undertaken by the National Institute of Economic and Social Research into reasons for purchasing imports rather than UK manufactured non-food goods.

1. Please tick the products in which you principally trade:

    Carpets

    China, earthenware and glassware

    Clothing: men's and boy's

    women's and girl's

    other including babywear

    Domestic electric appliances

    Domestic metalware

    Electronic consumer goods

    Food, drink and tobacco, CTN

    Footwear

    Furniture

    Household textiles and soft
       furnishings

    Leisure goods and sportswear

    Soap and toiletries

    Stationery and related products

    Toys and games

    Wallpaper and paint

    Other DIY goods

    Other consumer goods

2. As question 1 for large retailers on p. 121.

3. As question 2 for large retailers.

4. Are you: an independent retailer

    a branch of an enterprise with 2 to 9 outlets

    a branch of an enterprise with 10 or more outlets

5. Do you obtain goods for resale from:

> UK manufacturers and their agents
> Foreign manufacturers and their agents
> Importers
> Independent wholesalers
> Voluntary group and group wholesalers
> Cash-and-Carry
> Parent company's central or regional depot

Please tick any relevant suppliers.

NOTES AND REFERENCES

2 THE CONSUMER GOODS INDUSTRIES 1974–85

1 This figure is estimated from stock data in the Retail Enquiries, adjusted for changes in coverage and VAT and deflated by retail prices.
2 Estimates of total deliveries are based on incomplete data, grossed up by the DTI to allow for production by small firms. The grossing-up factors may not be wholly appropriate and can be large.
3 To give a correct measure of consumption or supplies available for consumption and trade (total supplies), stock changes should be added in, for example, consumption equals output *minus* changes in manufacturers' stocks *minus* exports *plus* imports *minus* changes in distributors' stocks.

3 THE STRUCTURE OF RETAILING IN THE UNITED KINGDOM

1 The retail sales index, which distinguishes small shops in terms of turnover rather than number of outlets, shows a different pattern of change but still a decline in the share of small shops. It is probably less reliable than the Retail Enquiries.
2 For details see Appendix 2.
3 There is virtually no published information about C. & A. Modes – the only major retailer that shrouds its operations in secrecy. Various trade estimates of its market share/turnover suggest that it has ranked in the top twenty throughout the period under review. Rough estimates of its turnover have been included in Appendix 2.
4 Monopolies and Mergers Commission (1983), The Great Universal Stores Plc and Empire Stores (Bradford) Plc, *Cmnd* 8777, London, HMSO.

4 THE BUYER'S POINT OF VIEW

1 House of Commons Industry and Trade Committee (1981), Report: Imports and exports, vol. II.
2 Since sterling was falling against the dollar and major West European currencies while questionnaires were being sent out and interviews undertaken, relative prices were moving in favour of United Kingdom producers, as was indicated in many interviews. The effects on price competition between British and foreign suppliers had not, however, fully worked through and comments on relative prices reflect a slightly less favourable rate of exchange.

5 CLOTHING AND KNITWEAR

1 The textile and clothing industries have indignantly rebutted the contention of the Silberston Report on 'The multi-fibre arrangement and the UK economy' (Department of Trade and Industry, 1984), that the MFA limits on imports from suppliers in developing countries merely caused a switch from restricted suppliers to others in Western Europe. So far as it goes this claim appears to be well-founded. It does not, however, meet the more serious objections to the MFA: that it increases prices to the consumer and bestows rents on both domestic and foreign producers, or on distributors.

6 DOMESTIC ELECTRIC APPLIANCES

1 For a discussion of the relation between scale and unit costs of production of refrigerators and washing machines in the major West European producing countries, see Owen, N. (1983), *Economies of Scale, Competitiveness and Trade Patterns within the European Community*, Oxford, Clarendon Press.
2 Monopolies and Mergers Commission (1983), London Electricity Board, *Cmnd* 8812, London, HMSO.
3 Monopolies and Mergers Commission (1981), Discounts to Retailers, *HC* 311, London, HMSO.
4 Price Commission (1976), *Small Electrical Appliances and Recommended Retail Prices*, London, HMSO.

7 HOUSEHOLD TEXTILES

1 Design Council (1983), Report to the Design Council on the Design of British Consumer Goods, July.

8 FURNITURE

1 *Financial Times*, 1 May, 1986. Some furniture manufacturers were ready and eager to supply Marks and Spencer, but part of their supplies come from a furniture factory taken over by an established supplier of *other* goods.

9 TOILETRIES; CHINA; WALL COVERINGS

1 The American majors have been here for many years. Some were initially established in the 1930s, when the United Kingdom offered both a promising home market and an export base; they continue to use plants in this country to supply overseas markets A great deal of foreign trade is thought to represent intra-firm transactions.
2 No statistical comparison of prices of domestic and imported products is possible since no information is available about quantities produced.
3 Design Council (1983), Report to the Design Council on the Design of British Consumer Goods, July.

10   CONCLUSION

1   House of Commons Industry and Trade Committee (1981), Report: Imports and exports, vol. II.

APPENDIX 2: TURNOVER OF MAJOR NON-FOOD RETAILERS 1976–84

1   Candidates for inclusion in 1984 included Clydesdale Retail Ltd, N. Brown Investments, Stead and Simpson and Wades. The latter was the subject of a management buyout in 1984.

INDEX OF PRODUCTS AND PROPER NAMES

RECENT PUBLICATIONS OF THE
NATIONAL INSTITUTE OF ECONOMIC
AND SOCIAL RESEARCH

published by
THE CAMBRIDGE UNIVERSITY PRESS

ECONOMIC AND SOCIAL STUDIES

OCCASIONAL PAPERS

NIESR STUDENTS' EDITION

Recent Publications

THE NATIONAL INSTITUTE OF ECONOMIC AND
SOCIAL RESEARCH

publishes regularly

THE NATIONAL INSTITUTE ECONOMIC REVIEW

A quarterly analysis of the general economic situation in the United Kingdom and the world overseas, with forecasts eighteen months ahead. The last issue each year contains an assessment of medium-term prospects. There are also in most issues special articles on subjects of interest to academic and business economists.

Annual subcriptions £45.00 (home), and £60.00 (abroad), also single issues for the current year. £12.50 (home) and £18.00 (abroad), are available directly from NIESR, 2 Dean Trench Street, Smith Square, London, SWIP 3HE.

Subscriptions at the special reduced price of £18.00 p.a. are available to students in the United Kingdom and Irish Republic on application to the Secretary of the Institute.

Back numbers and reprints of issues which have gone out of stock are distributed by Wm. Dawson and Sons Ltd., Cannon House, Park Farm Road, Folkestone. Microfiche copies for the years 1959–85 are available from EP Microform Ltd. Bradford Road, East Ardsley, Wakefield, Yorks.

Published by
HEINEMANN EDUCATIONAL BOOKS
GOWER PUBLISHING COMPANY

DEMAND MANAGEMENT
Edited by MICHAEL POSNER. 1978. pp. 256. £6.50 (paperback) net.
DE-INDUSTRIALISATION
Edited by FRANK BLACKABY. 1979. pp. 282. £12.95 (paperback) net.
BRITAIN IN EUROPE
Edited by WILLIAM WALLACE. 1980. pp. 224. £8.50 (paperback) net.
THE FUTURE OF PAY BARGAINING
Edited by FRANK BLACKABY. 1980. pp. 246. £16.00 (hardback), £7.50 (paperback) net.
INDUSTRIAL POLICY AND INNOVATION
Edited by CHARLES CARTER. 1981. pp. 241. £18.50 (hardback), £7.50 (paperback) net.
THE CONSTITUTION OF NORTHERN IRELAND
Edited by DAVID WATT, 1981. pp. 227. £19.50 (hardback), £9.50 (paperback) net.
RETIREMENT POLICY. THE NEXT FIFTY YEARS
Edited by MICHAEL FOGARTY. 1982. pp. 224. £17.50 (hardback), £7.50 (paperback) net.
SLOWER GROWTH IN THE WESTERN WORLD
Edited by R.C.O. MATTHEWS. 1982. pp. 182. £19.50 (hardback), £9.50 (paperback) net.
NATIONAL INTERESTS AND LOCAL GOVERNMENT
Edited by KEN YOUNG. 1983. pp. 180. £17.50 (hardback), £9.50 (paperback) net.
EMPLOYMENT, OUTPUT AND INFLATION
Edited by A.J.C. BRITTON. 1983. pp. 208. £25.00 net.
THE TROUBLED ALLIANCE, ATLANTIC RELATIONS IN THE 1980s
Edited by LAWRENCE FREEDMAN. 1983. pp. 176. £19.50 (hardback), £7.50 (paperback) net.
EDUCATION AND ECONOMIC PERFORMANCE
Edited by G.D.N. WORSWICK. 1984. pp. 152. £18.50 net.
ENERGY SELF-SUFFICIENCY FOR THE UK
Edited by ROBERT BELGRAVE. 1985. pp. 224. £19.50 net.
THE FUTURE OF BRITISH DEFENCE POLICY
Edited by JOHN ROPER. 1985. pp. 205. £18.50 net.
ENERGY MANAGEMENT: CAN WE LEARN FROM OTHERS?
By G.F. RAY. 1985. pp. 120. £19.50 net.
UNEMPLOYMENT AND LABOUR MARKET POLICIES
Edited by P.E. HART. 1986. pp. 230. £19.50 net.
NEW PRIORITIES IN PUBLIC SPENDING
Edited by M.S. LEVITT. 1987. pp. 136. £17.50 net.